"Where do you come from?"

Hitler refugees
in Great Britain
then and now:
The happy compromise!

Carl F. Flesch

Pen Press Publishers Ltd
London

Copyright © Carl F Flesch 2001

All rights reserved

No part of this publication may be reproduced, stored
in a retrieval system, or transmitted in any form
or by any means, without the prior permission
in writing of the publisher.

First published in Great Britain by
Pen Press Publishers Ltd
39-41, North Road
Islington
London N7 9DP

ISBN 1 900796 79 1

Printed and bound in the UK

A catalogue record of this book is available
from the British Library

Cover design by
John Minnion

For my children, grandchildren and great-grandchildren
and
in memory of my beloved wife Ruth, who shared so many of my experiences.

By the same author:

'...and do you also play the violin?'

Inside Insurance

Contents

Foreword vii

About this book ix

Then and now 1

Early days 7

'Some of my best friends ..' 34

Language, humour, names and all that 62

Customs, morals and similar matters 81

War 96

Relations with Germany and Germans after the war ... 128

In particular... 148
    Refugees and the monarchy 150
    Racism 159
    Once more – language! 164
    Children of refugees 167
    Attitude to work 171
    Refugee organisations 175
    Nationality 186
    Thank you Britain fund 187

So, what next? 190

Foreword

This is a book of reflections and reminiscences that has, I believe, qualities and insights of real value to offer its readers. When Carl Flesch asked me to write a foreword to it, I was pleased and flattered. Flattered because the foreword to his previous book, a son's view of his famous violinist father entitled, with becoming modesty, *And do you also play the violin?,* has been written by the late Lord Menuhin. And pleased because into this book has been distilled the wisdom and experience of ninety years, one quarter of which was spent in pre-Hitler Germany and the rest in England as a refugee, then as an increasingly but never entirely assimilated immigrant.

There have been academic studies of the refugees from Hitler who settled in Great Britain after 1933, and there have also appeared in recent years any number of autobiographical accounts by former refugees from Central Europe recounting their experiences before and after emigration to this country. Carl Flesch's book fills a gap between these two types of books. On the one hand, it has a great deal of the immediacy and vividness of the autobiographical accounts, based as it is on direct personal experience, but it takes the form of a series of chapters, each presenting reflections on important aspects of the refugee experience, not straight personal history. On the other hand, it is not burdened with the academic style, with the jargon, footnotes and learned apparatus that characterise works of pure scholarship, but it nevertheless succeeds in marshalling evidence, deploying cogent arguments and reaching serious conclusions about the experiences and development of the refugee community that settled in Britain after 1933.

Combining a chronological approach to the years after 1933 with reflections about certain key areas of refugee life – especially about relations with that curious breed, the British – Carl Flesch employs a punchy style and an agreeable dry sense of humour in his book. His conclusions are clearly stated, sometimes controversial (as on the subject of the bombing of the extermination camps), and always highly readable. This is a book that contributes in an important way to our understanding of the refugee experience, and it conjures up perceptively and humorously the long process of adjustment that led the erstwhile refugees to reach their 'happy compromise' with their British hosts.

Anthony Grenville

About this book

Not very long ago I placed a telephone order with a shop. After my first sentence the young girl at the other end of the line asked: 'Are you German?'

'Well, I was, many years ago.'

'I thought so,' she said and proceeded to continue the conversation in German. Now, sometimes you come across a foreign shop assistant who, being away from home, may be pleased to have the opportunity of talking in her own language for a change. But this girl was quite obviously British-born and her German, though good, was by no means perfect.

To say that I was irritated would be an understatement. I have been living in Great Britain for more than two thirds of my life. While I know that my accent is not perfect – unless you have been in this country from school age onwards, this is a practical impossibility, even for trained actors – I flatter myself that it is no longer what is usually termed 'foreign'. As a matter of fact, in a German's case it need not necessarily be the accent that gives the game away, but rather the difference in the intonation between the two languages, which is somehow harsher in German than in English.

The girl on the telephone was obviously highly pleased with herself and the way she had handled the situation. Not only had she 'put a foreigner at his ease' (or so she thought) but she had at the same time been able to show off her skills to her own satisfaction. If, by any chance, she should read this, I regret that she is in for a disappointment: her employers lost me as a customer. An over-reaction, I know, and on the facts of the case completely unjustified, but I make no apologies. If people like her only knew how misguided they are! She clearly did not have the slightest inkling of how annoying, not to say hurtful, her behaviour was. Someone who, for many years, has been living in a country where he was not born but which he has gained citizenship of and feels fully committed to, cannot help being irritated if he is recognised as an 'alien' the moment he opens his mouth. Clearly, all his efforts to learn to speak and pronounce English correctly have been in vain. His deficiencies are being shown up and he is being talked down to with obvious condescension, however kindly meant. The effect is bound to be upsetting and depressing.

This incident, though very minor in itself, set me thinking. How have we former refugees from Nazi oppression realistically got on? What are the 'natives' ' true feelings about us, and vice versa? The numerous books dealing with emigration from Germany after Hitler had seized power give, to my knowledge, comparatively little information on this particular aspect. The reason is, of course, that most stories are strictly autobiographical and have been written with the intention of relating the author's personal experiences instead of those of refugees as a body.

There are, on the one hand, memoirs by very prominent former refugees. To us, their fellow immigrants, these are usually fascinating and a cause for pride, because they demonstrate that some of us managed to be very successful in spite of the disadvantages under which we laboured when we started in this country. For the general reader, however, the author's origins are of minor importance. He is concerned with the writer's history and achievements. These are what make the book interesting for him. He would not buy it just to read about matters that have little or nothing to do with the author's present position and successes and the way they came about.

On the other hand there are those memoirs whose value lies precisely in the remarkable stories their authors have to tell about their individual experiences as Jewish refugees from Nazi oppression and the persecutions and struggles before and after emigration. The position they eventually gained in the community is almost incidental – in the majority of cases it will not be substantially different from that of most other immigrants. These books are, understandably, usually of greater interest to us, their fellow refugees, than to the general public. There are exceptions: the world-wide reaction to the Anne Frank Diaries is the most notable example. However, this certainly cannot be regarded as anything like typical.

But whichever category these books belong to, they are, by their very nature, usually very personal accounts. Few attempts seem to have been made to address the *general* questions: How did we new arrivals feel? Where have we former refugees got to? How did we get there? And where do we go from here?

These are very complicated questions. This book does not seek to give anywhere near a full answer; that will one day have to be the task of a fully qualified sociologist.* But it attempts to make a modest contribution

---

* In this connection I would like to mention an article by Dr Anthony Grenville, entitled 'German-speaking Exiles in Great Britain' in the *Yearbook of the Research Centre for German and Austrian Exile Studies*, Vol 1 (1999). Dr Grenville is also working on a book about 'AJR Information', the monthly publication by the Association of Jewish Refugees from Germany, Austria and other Nazi-occupied countries.

towards beginning to fill a gap which to my mind exists. What I have to say makes no claim to being in any way learned, profound or exhaustive. It represents simply – and hopefully not without humour – the observations of an average former refugee who has no personal story to tell that could be important to anyone but himself: I left Germany shortly after Hitler had come to power and therefore was spared the harrowing experiences of those who were unable to escape until a later stage. Thank God, none of my immediate family perished in the Holocaust. Like everybody else, I was initially not allowed to work and therefore had to live very frugally but, thanks to help from my parents, I was fortunate enough never to know real financial hardship. For these reasons I feel able to concentrate in this book on the far more interesting theme of us, the 'first generation refugees' of the 1930s, as a group; and not least on our slow integration – as far as it went – into this country at various stages.

Whilst this is in no way intended as a book of memoirs, it inevitably contains many personal recollections. Where they are included, the reason is not that I consider them remarkable as such (however important they may have been to me) but that they seemed to me to be typical: undoubtedly many of my fellow refugees experienced similar thoughts and events.

However, this is not all I have had in mind in writing this book. I am reminded of the late Artur Schnabel, not only a world renowned pianist but also deservedly famous for his many *bons mots*. Referring to the fact that piano recitals often fall into two groups, 'heavy' classical music before and lighter bonbons after the interval – a practice which he abhorred and never followed himself – he used to say: 'Most recitals are boring during the first and entertaining during the second half. In my concerts, both halves are equally boring.' In a way I intend to reverse this format: I shall have the 'heavier' stuff at the end.

I am going to try and draw, from the somewhat haphazardly anecdotal, a few general conclusions regarding other issues, especially the subject of 'class' which is so much hyped today. I believe I have discovered, not without surprise, that the specific category of 'refugees' leads to some possibly new insights into the class question. I can only hope that Artur Schnabel's remarks will not apply to this book!

So while I said a few paragraphs earlier that this is not a learned book, it does reach certain verdicts. Some readers may not agree with them at all; they may even consider them to be mistaken. They could well be right. But if they are, my excuse is that during the last one or two decades (and before) so much nonsense has been said and written about the subject of class and Britain's 'classless society', that a little more cannot possibly hurt!

But back to our original subject. Clearly, sooner rather than later, none of us original refugees will be left. Let's face it: experience shows that by no means all our descendants, confronted as they are with their own present problems, are overly concerned with our past ones. Is there then any point in recounting them? I believe the answer is 'yes'. The difficulties of immigration go beyond those of their particular period. In the present state of the world, large population movements are an on-going phenomenon. There will be refugees and immigrants for a long time to come. And whilst many of their circumstances and characteristics will obviously differ from those of refugees from Naziism and, for that matter, from one another, there will still remain sufficient problems applicable to all of them. Hence, relating our experiences should be of general interest. It might even serve a practical purpose. I would not be surprised if some of the matters touched upon in this book will be of increasing importance in the future.

There remained one problem, admittedly of a somewhat commercial nature. Like every author I would like people to read what I have written. Since during the past few decades more and more books about refugees have been published, some with very intriguing titles indeed, there was – no, is – the obvious possibility of potential readers dismissing mine with 'Oh God, not another one!' How could I, in my title, convey the fact that this one is an attempt to approach the subject in a different (I do not claim better) way without at the same time incurring the risk of possibly being misleading to the reader? I can only hope that my eventual solution has achieved both its positive and negative objects.

Finally, I'd like to express my thanks to a number of people: Anthony Grenville for his invaluable advice and encouragement; Bina Wallach for her most valuable contributions; Terry Stone for so carefully vetting my manuscript; my publishers and their editor Linda Lloyd for their patience and support; Paul M Cohn, Otto Deutsch, Judy Glaser, Martin Hassock, Renate Herzog, Eric Joyce, A Kirsen, Charles Leigh, J Nina Lieberman, Robert Miller, Ann Ollrom, Henry Rado, Dr E Rosenstiel, Inge Samson, A Saville, Erwin Schneider, Herbert Sutton and H Tunwell for the trouble they took in contributing material to the 'Humour' chapter. (Should I have overlooked anybody, my apologies!). Last but not least, I want to thank my family for their interest and in particular my daughter Carol Wine for the considerable trouble she took and her valuable suggestions, gratefully though perhaps not always graciously received.

With all that help I am beginning to wonder how much of this book has really been written by me!

Anyway, here it is.

Then and now

It is obvious that we refugees from Nazi Germany must, both by assimilation and by passage of time, have become very different people from those we were when we first arrived in this country in the 1930s. But what is easily forgotten is that, during that period, Great Britain itself underwent very fundamental changes. The peaceful country in which we found refuge almost two generations ago is in a great many ways simply no longer comparable to what it has become through social and other developments and upheavals, many of which originated in, or were accelerated by, the Second World War and its aftermath.

At the time it was an island in more senses than one. It could be reached practically only by sea, something that frequently meant a pretty uncomfortable and stressful journey. This comparative isolation was undoubtedly one of the reasons why it was so 'insular', so very different from the Continental countries to whom most of the British, with their nation still a world power, felt vastly superior. It was very rare for one of its citizens to talk it down, as happens so frequently today. As a result, we immigrants respected this attitude of superiority almost without question. That is to say, while we might have been critical of certain matters, customs and opinions, there were considerably more that impressed us greatly. I feel this country is likely to appear to any foreigner in a far less impressive light today than it did to us, to whom it was the 'promised land' which we had been very fortunate and relieved to be allowed to enter. This was bound to influence our general attitude. If the natives of a country are not critical of it, new arrivals are unlikely to find too many faults of their own accord. Strange customs – yes; open to strong criticism – normally no.

Some of the national characteristics immediately apparent to us were, for instance, the general courtesy – people colliding in the street, no matter which 'class' they belonged to, would both automatically say 'sorry' at the same moment, a habit so very different from the more common reaction we had been used to in our homeland. There, we would have been more likely to hear something like an angry 'Can't you look where you're going, you fool!'

We noticed the (today almost unimaginable) quiet atmosphere in restaurants as opposed to the noise in Continental establishments; the absence of pushing in a queue and, for that matter, the custom of automatically forming one. Speakers' Corner in Hyde Park with its often weird performers and good-natured audience, which normally required just one or two policemen to curb any occasional over-enthusiasm, was a revelation, something that would have been unthinkable in most other countries. It was one of the sights of London we considered worth reporting in letters home. We marvelled at the London Bobbies, unarmed, friendly and helpful servants of the public, so very different from our perception of the German policeman, strictly a representative of public authority and showing it on every suitable or unsuitable occasion. We noted the full accessibility of Government quarters, including Downing Street – no barricades. Then there was the fact that many residents did not in the least worry about leaving their front doors unlocked, the risk of possible intruders simply not entering their minds. People of all ages and both sexes went out at night without giving a thought to possible muggers – and so on.

All this appeared to us far more important, and rightly so, than the occasionally strange-seeming customs and attitudes, some of which I shall be discussing in their appropriate contexts. Those were the good old days, never, I fear, to return!

In view of the perceived vast superiority of the British over us, the idea that we ourselves might one day be able to contribute something of value did not occur to most of us unless we belonged to the chosen few, mostly in the worlds of art and science, whose fame and reputation had preceded them and who were received with open arms, representing, as it were, a welcome by-product of the German persecution. They were therefore accepted not with reluctance or condescension, but considered as actually worth competing for. These, though, were far from typical refugees. There was very little doubt that the modest opinion most of us had of ourselves was shared by our hosts. At that time the certainty that 'British is best' was well-nigh axiomatic. The British tendency for understatement definitely did not extend to the almost touching self-belief – or should I say self-deception? – expressed by prominent people and in the press.

Let me give a few examples*:

---

* I am taking them from a book by GJ Renier, published by Williams and Norgate Ltd in 1931 and re-published by Ernest Benn Ltd in 1956. Today it is out of print, largely forgotten and not easy to get hold of, but at the time it achieved no fewer than 14 reprints. This success may in part have been due to its very cheeky title: *The English, Are They Human?*, but there is no doubt that it offered a number of valuable insights into the English character and conditions of life at the time, as seen by a foreigner who was not a refugee but had chosen of his own free will to live and work in England. While, in my view, the author on occasion sounds somewhat

'We own the brightest posters and gayest underground stations in Europe' (*Star*, 18/6/1920. At that time the word 'gay' did not, of course, have its present meaning).

'I met a man yesterday who has travelled halfway across the world, to find that the greatest wonder of the world is – the Englishwoman! He is the Sultan of Zanzibar.' (*Sunday Express* 9/6/1929.)

'The most famous piece of statuary in the world ... [is the] ... fountain ... surmounted by the statue of Eros in Piccadilly Circus.' (*Sunday Express* 20/10/1929).

'England has more beautiful and valuable pictures than any other country in the world.'* (*Evening Standard* 12/6/1929)

'The British Post Office is one of the few wonders of the world ...' (Notes, Organ of Association of Head Postmasters, December 1929) Of course, to paraphrase Mandy Rice-Davis on a later occasion: 'They would say that, wouldn't they?'

'The British Press, taken as a whole, is the best, the fairest ambivalent, the opinions he expresses are free from the inferiority complex so often experienced by the typical refugee whose self-esteem is affected by his precarious position. Thus it sometimes provides useful independent confirmation of our own opinions. I am sure that the author's choice of examples dating from 1929/30, ie a few years before the German refugee immigration began, is irrelevant, because there had been no perceptible change in British conditions during the intervening years.

Incidentally, the reaction to the book by the typical British citizen could be one of considerable annoyance. I remember lending it in all innocence to a British lady as a good read. She never spoke to me again.

* This is neatly matched by the opinion expressed by the art critic and scholar John Hunt (1775-1849): 'Rembrandt is not to be compared in the painting of character with our extraordinarily gifted English artist, Mr Rippingille.' (*The Cassell Dictionary of Unfortunate Quotations*, 1999) and the cleanest Press in the world.' (Stanley Baldwin 24/6/1930)

'The best waiters in the world are the fully qualified English ones.' (*Evening Standard* 22/2/1930)

'The middle-aged Englishman, travelled and moderately wealthy, is the greatest gourmet in the world, better even than the French.' (*Evening Standard* 19/3/1930)

'British cooks are the best in Europe ... We did not find an honest British bun anywhere in Europe ... Greek and Viennese bakers were greatly impressed by the Eccles cake, currant buns and mince-pies ...' (Spokesman for the National Association of Master Bakers, Confectioners and Caterers, 1929).

'Let us cure ourselves of the habit of pretending that the British climate is the worst in the world. In fact, it is the best in the world.' (*Sunday Express* 14/7/29)

Enough of that. I am not here to comment. My intention is to write about German and Austrian refugees, not British social history. Some of the opinions quoted, whilst hardly defensible today, may have been more true 70 years ago. Whatever the case, they show a nation at that time unconditionally convinced of its superiority in practically everything, and not shy to express this opinion loudly, clearly and unambiguously as a self-evident truth. How else could *The Manchester Guardian* have written, on 16/1/1930: 'We are the most self-deprecating people on earth.' I can only assume that the author was a comparative newcomer to the world of journalism and not exactly interested in anything his colleagues had written, otherwise he could hardly have missed the examples I have just given.

Looking back, I cannot exactly remember how we reacted consciously to this constant refrain of self-congratulation; but subconsciously, since we were already conditioned to think extremely highly of England, we found little of it particularly questionable, except perhaps the remarks about the British climate and English cooking. Of course, most of us were not particularly avid newspaper readers at the time, but these opinions, constantly reiterated, were bound to be reflected in the attitude of the average British citizen. It is clear that this must have contributed to our strong subliminal conditioning and thereby have had a profound influence on our views.

Thus, if we talk about our early days, we have to remember that in a great many respects we spent them in what can almost be called a different country from present-day Britain, and with people vastly more self-confident and self-opinionated than they are today. It is an intriguing question whether we would have felt and fared markedly differently if conditions had been the same then as they are now. Well, we shall never know, though the attitude of many of today's immigrants does give an indication.

Early days

I don't know the exact numbers, but when I arrived in London early in 1934, refugees were still a trickle compared with the flood that came later on. It was, for instance, still possible for the Hon. Mrs Franklin, a member of a wealthy, long-established Jewish banking family, to give, without having to worry about overcrowding her splendid Bayswater home, regular receptions offering generous hospitality to any refugee who wanted to attend. People who had known each other in their homeland but had lost touch were often reunited in this way. We were all supplied with name tags and many new friendships originated on these occasions. I myself remember them with immense affection: it was there that I met the girl who later became my wife.

The official refugee centre was Woburn House, which was mostly staffed by volunteers and concerned itself to the best of its abilities with helping us, including, where necessary, offering financial support. It was usually the first port of call for anybody who was in trouble or in need of advice generally. One of its vital tasks was to assist in getting the relatives of refugees out of Germany and into England. It also took it upon itself to make as certain as possible that we did not unintentionally cause offence to our British hosts. To this end it issued a booklet enumerating a number of Dos and Don'ts (as, incidentally, did the Home Office, making recommendations to British citizens about how to react to us). On the whole I believe we were well behaved and caused little concern or trouble to the natives or the authorities. When we did, it was probably due more to our inexperience than to intentional transgressions. The important part Woburn House played in the lives of so many of us, particularly in the beginning, should never be forgotten. There is no need to say more: its history, activities and achievements are too well documented to need repetition here

It is no doubt a truism that any refugee's social and economic status on arrival in his new country is usually two to three levels below that which he occupied at home. For most of us, with very few exceptions, this meant starting on the lower ground floor of society. Many refugees had next to no money, a time-limited visa, no labour permit let alone a job, whether paid or unpaid, no British friends or acquaintances to speak of, and often only the barest minimum of linguistic knowledge. Additionally, most of them were saddled with the desperate worry about the dangerous situation of members of their families who had not yet succeeded in leaving Germany: clearly, by any standard, a near-desperate situation.

Yet, unlikely though this may sound, I – as do many others with whom I have discussed this phenomenon from time to time – look back on this period of my life as a basically happy one. During these early days, the decision to emigrate was easier for people who had least to lose at home, and this meant that the majority of us were young. We were all equal and shared the firm hope that our fortunes would one day improve (they could not really sink much lower). Subconsciously we must have given each other far greater moral support than we realised at the time.

A few suicides did unfortunately occur but I believe they did not exceed the British average; as far as I know, very few were directly due to the hopelessness of an individual's situation as such. In course of time there were a few notable ones – for instance, those of the writers Stefan Zweig and Kurt Tucholsky – but they were due mainly to despair about world conditions in general.

The attitude of the typical refugee was on the whole positive. We eagerly grasped every opportunity of discussing and comparing our difficulties and worries, gladly accepting advice from people whose position in our homeland might have been distinctly inferior to ours, but who proved to be either luckier or more streetwise than we were. Nobody had to be ashamed of his or her present lowly situation. This made for a kind of camaraderie that is difficult to describe, let alone explain to those who have not experienced it. With the exception of deliberate 'assimilators' with whom I shall be dealing presently, most of us lived closely together in the same districts – principally Hampstead – frequented the same establishments (as far as we could find the money to visit them) and faced our difficulties, especially the bar on doing any work, with as much gallows humour as we could muster.

Inevitably, some people did not strictly keep to the job restriction and illegally accepted work – any work, freelance or regular employment – at very low pay. And unsurprisingly there were virtually penniless refugees who were only too glad to avail themselves of the opportunity to pay lower prices for certain services if they needed them. This could lead to precarious situations. I heard of a German dentist who at that time had neither the permission nor the British qualifications to practise, but who occasionally and clandestinely did so all the same. One day he had just extracted a patient's tooth when the doorbell rang. He threw all his equipment into a little suitcase, somewhat in the manner of Del Boy in 'Only fools and horses', ushered his patient out via the back stairs and uttered the classic if not strictly professional admonition: 'If you start bleeding, don't come back!' German doctors, too, who had to study anew in order to obtain British qualifications were often glad to dispense unofficial medical advice just to keep their hand in.

Getting a labour permit was a major achievement and people who had obtained one were generally admired and envied. The question 'How did you do it?' occasionally produced somewhat unorthodox answers. Some people had rather strange views on how to go about it. I shall relate one example later, since it happened to involve me personally.

Social distinctions did not exist. I remember being a regular guest at a restaurant frequented mainly by refugees. On one occasion I asked the waitress, a refugee like myself, but not known to me socially, what soups there were on the menu that day.

'Tomato and minestrone,' she told me.

'I'll have the minestrone.'

'No, take the tomato, it's better today.'

'OK, tomato then.'

After a few minutes she re-appeared with minestrone, which she placed before me without comment.

'But I thought I ordered tomato?' I said diffidently.

'I changed my mind,' she shrugged. (It sounds still better in German: 'Ich hab' mich umentschlossen'.) We all found this funny, and no-one considered this lack of social differentiation in any way inappropriate or offensive.

Of course, all this did not, could not, last. As more and more immigrants succeeded in getting a foothold of some sort, as some began to be more successful than others, class distinctions and even snobbery reappeared and the – for want of a better word – 'idyllic' state of affairs vanished, only to reappear in a similar guise and comparatively briefly during the darkest days of World War II. But that is a different story with which I shall be dealing in its proper place.

I referred earlier to the equality of status 'with very few exceptions'. There were mainly three. The simplest one I have already mentioned elsewhere: refugees outstanding in their profession whom the British regarded as a 'catch' and to whom they offered every facility by way of unrestricted residence permission and labour permit. They were in a class by themselves, surrounded as they were from their arrival by British people and in no need of financial and little need of moral support.

Then there were 'Pass-Engländer', passport Englishmen who were lucky enough to be British by birth. Like ourselves, they had usually hitherto spent all their life outside Great Britain and were as German or Austrian as the rest of us, except that they happened to have been born on British soil – possibly on holiday or even on a British boat – or their parents had, at the crucial time for some reason, possessed a British passport. Whether or not they already had some connections in this country, they needed neither residence nor labour permit and could accept any job offered to them. They fell into two categories: those who tried to be genuinely helpful to their less fortunate fellow refugees and those who did the opposite.

As it happened, I encountered both types: quite a number for whose help I shall always be abundantly grateful, and one or two whom I remember with considerably less pleasure. One in particular, a member of the latter group, was a cartoonist who in spite of being British had so far been unsuccessful in getting his work accepted by any British paper. Consequently he was as impecunious as the rest of us. We became quite friendly and, since he had so little money, he began regularly to drop in on me during meal times and, with my permission, to use my boarding house room during part of the day when I was out, in order to save himself the pennies needed to feed the gas meter at his own abode.

One day he asked me whether I could lend him some money, £3, coupled with the promise of repayment within a few days. I was in the lucky position of receiving a modest allowance from my parents, but could certainly not spare this amount for any length of time. Hence, when nothing, not even a mention or excuse, happened at the due date, I had to remind him of his promise and, after some time, to press him for the return of the loan. I got no response until one day he informed me coolly that if I did not stop bothering him, he would report me to the Home Office for 'molesting an Englishman'.

This naturally signalled the end of a beautiful friendship but what was significant, and typical of our perceived precarious refugee status at that time, was the fact that I took this threat entirely seriously: I not only immediately abandoned any effort to regain my badly-needed £3, but in great alarm sought the advice of Woburn House against what I regarded as a serious danger. They promised to help should it become necessary, but of course the threat never materialised. Luckily, people of this man's ilk were the exception.

The third category were those people who had decided from the word 'go' to try and drop any connection with their fellow immigrants' circles and institutions in order to become, as it were, 'fully paid-up members' of the British community as soon as possible. These 'instant assimilators' raised rather more complicated questions, albeit mainly of a psychological nature. They usually already had some British connections, were therefore not as dependent on the advice or moral support of their fellow refugees as we were, and deliberately avoided any contact with us. Looking back, there was not really any good reason why we should blame them for this. If you want to acclimatise to a foreign country and learn its language and customs as quickly as possible, the most efficient way, apart from acquiring a native girl- or boyfriend (unless he or she wants to learn *your* language), is to seek and cultivate social contacts with as many citizens of the host country as you possibly can. But it does require several qualities of mind not everybody possesses: self-confidence (will there be full acceptance by the British?); a certain amount of ruthlessness and lack of loyalty, enabling you to shed the warmth and comfort of long-standing friendships, either for a certain period or forever; and the willingness to cut yourself off from the roots and cultural traditions of your native country.

There is, as I have said, nothing wrong with all that if you are so minded. In fact none of us were interested in retaining any connection with German 'culture' at that point – but when we experienced in my circle one or two examples of a hitherto intimate friend acting in this way, I have to admit that most of us regarded his attitude as hurtful, disloyal, snobbish and self-seeking. This throws a significant light on our own mental attitude at the time though not necessarily on the correctness of our views.

I shall revert to this intriguing subject of assimilation (or, perhaps, 'non-assimilation') in its proper context.

To return to the job question. This was a double whammy. If a refugee succeeded in getting the offer of a job, the next obstacle was getting the labour permit for it. You had to motivate your future employer to apply for it – the prospective employee could not do so himself. Owing to substantial unemployment prevalent in Great Britain at that time, no foreigner was permitted to take a job that might deprive a British-born citizen of a chance to work. Fair enough! So we had to show qualifications or skills not possessed by Englishmen. It has to be gratefully put on record that this rule was subject to a good deal of flexibility. I believe that, had it been strictly applied, few of us would have found work. There was, after all, very little we could really do better than our British contemporaries except of course speak German – not a skill very much in demand at that time and definitely not a sellers' market.

Unfortunately not many prospective employers were prepared to go to any great trouble and apply themselves seriously to the task of obtaining the services of someone with rather doubtful special skills. If they did show willingness, the reason was frequently not their belief in our unique capabilities but the realistic consideration that we were prepared to work for very low wages or even – those of us who could afford it – as unpaid 'trainees' just in order to get back into the swim or learn a new trade or skill. Another reason could have been that a refugee might well be less troublesome than a British employee.

When we did land a job, our employers' attitudes to us could be somewhat mixed. They all were aware of our precarious position. Some, though not many, regarded employing us as genuine charity and took an almost paternal interest in our well-being, even to the extent of overlooking the fact that our work was by no means always up to the promised scratch. Others adopted the opposite view and took, sometimes quite shamelessly, every advantage they could. They knew that we were most unlikely to walk out of our own volition, for the labour permit was valid only for the job with that particular employer and any change meant beginning the whole rigmarole of applying anew. The best-known examples of this were female refugees who were usually allowed into this country only on condition that they accepted jobs as domestics. The trials of some of these unfortunates have been the subject of a number of autobiographies; some spiced with a good deal of humour. For obvious reasons I have no personal experience.

But between those two extremes, employers often showed very little understanding. Any unexpected obstacle or complication and they would drop us like as hot brick. I myself had a harrowing experience of this kind. I had been recommended to a prominent firm of Lloyd's brokers who had agreed to apply for a labour permit for me as an unpaid trainee. I got the permit – mine was a comparatively clear case and the procedure took 'only' ten weeks – and got on quite well in the firm, or so I thought.

But one day, after a few months, I was summoned into the presence of my boss who informed me without ceremony that I was being dismissed without notice.

'Why, for heaven's sake, what have I done?'
'You have been spying.'
'Spying? Me? In what way?'

'You have been reading our clients' files.'

'Of course I've been reading files. That's what I'm here for. I've sometimes even been asked to help translating letters to or from Germany.'

But whatever I said fell on deaf ears. The one concession I was granted was to be allowed to stay until Christmas – not a big deal since we were already in mid-December. However, I desperately grasped at that straw, for if I lost this position, the British authorities might have got it into their heads that my 'training' had been completed, consider that there was no reason for me to remain in this country and ship me back to Germany. Or they might have done so because of my alleged misconduct. This was not a prospect to be relished: refugees returning to Germany were bound to be the Nazis' most obvious targets.

I could not remotely imagine what had caused this ludicrous accusation and extraordinarily unfair treatment. Eventually it dawned on me: the firm had extensive and lucrative German connections and shortly after my arrival a second trainee had put in an appearance – the son of an important German client. I had taken good care to ensure that our paths crossed as little as possible and our mutual attitude had been one of distant politeness. However, undoubtedly this boy had made it his business to report to his father post-haste that his London insurance brokers were employing a German Jew who might have access to his firm's files – clearly an impossible situation from a Nazi-German's point of view.

The father's reaction was foreseeable – a strong letter of complaint to the British firm, possibly even coupled with an ultimatum as to what would happen if my employment were not terminated forthwith. I can fully appreciate that keeping an important client on the books had to take precedence over the fate of an insignificant young refugee to whom the firm was under no particular obligation. However, the point of the story is not the fact of my dismissal, but the way in which it was carried out. My employers demonstrated not only a lack of understanding generally, but also an indifference concerning my fate in particular and the very serious consequences the episode might have had both for my safety and my future career. With that 'track record' how could I ever hope to obtain any future employment?

I do not have sufficient evidence to form a definite opinion, but some stories I heard from friends make me believe that my experience of employers' attitudes was not unique. Even in cases where the hiring of a refugee might have been regarded as an act of kindness and given the employer a nice feeling of moral superiority, if difficulties of any kind cropped up the original idea was forgotten and any pretence of sympathy abandoned. It was not unlike children getting a puppy for Christmas and, once they realise that all is not pure joy, thoughtlessly abandoning it. My ex-boss was obviously not troubled by any bad conscience. Many years later this man who had dismissed me so unfairly died at a ripe old age. The trade papers brought fulsome obituaries, stressing *inter alia* his charitable work and the way in which he had habitually looked after people in need. Fortunately, at that stage, I could afford an indulgent smile.

At the time, however, there was nothing for it but immediately to become a 'student' of some sort. Accordingly I enrolled in a 'School of Advertising' run by an advertising agent *manqué* – the most useless few months

I have ever spent in my life, but I was temporarily safe. At the same time I applied for a labour permit as a freelance insurance broker. The way in which I went about this shows the typical inexperience of refugees generally and, as already indicated, the weird ideas current among us at the time.

Since our numbers during that period were still comparatively small, the authorities took it upon themselves to go into these applications with far greater care than they did later when figures had risen to the tens of thousands. Accordingly a young plain clothes Scotland Yard detective was assigned to my case and went fully into every aspect of my circumstances, financial as well as personal. Everything seemed to stand up satisfactorily and I had the highest hopes. However, well-meaning friends threw a considerable spanner into the works: 'You'll have to bribe that man,' they warned me, 'otherwise your chances are nil.' Quite apart from the fact that I saw no reason for this – I felt that everything had gone splendidly – I had always thought that England was one of the few countries where the offer of a bribe was not only unnecessary but in fact highly dangerous. Moreover, I was the most unsuitable person imaginable for attempting to bribe anyone. However, my friends insisted and seemed to me to have far greater experience in these matters than I, so eventually I came to the conclusion that there was nothing for it but to follow their advice.

But how to go about it? After a lot of worrying, I decided on a highly diplomatic approach: 'You have been so very kind to me during the last few days that I feel I should give you a little present to remember me by. But I have no idea what you would like. If you would not consider it a bribe I would suggest as the most suitable solution giving you some money so that you can buy something for yourself.'

Breathless pause. I saw myself already arrested and deported. I shall never forget the officer's laconic reply: 'Chance it.' Relieved, I gave him an enormous amount: three guineas, more than my living expenses for one week and definitely a larger amount than I could really afford. But desperate circumstances called for desperate measures.

So I awaited the outcome with considerable confidence. The application was declined! This raises a number of interesting questions: could the British police of the time be bribed or not? If so, did the officer accept the money in this way or as the harmless gift I had suggested? Probably the former: but in that case, should my application not have been successful? Perhaps he had intended to teach me a lesson? Or had he considered the amount risibly low? It certainly had not been for me. Obviously, I don't know the answers to this day, nor whether both the officer and I committed any offence. If we did, I am hoping that after more than 65 years no further action will be taken. But looking back, I consider myself lucky that my gullibility and inexperience did not cause me severe difficulties at the time, as they might easily have done.

At any rate, having been unsuccessful with my application, I had to try again. Through my family I had close connections with the world of music and was therefore better able than most to assess the insurance requirements of professional musicians. They are somewhat special and different from those of members of other callings. Luckily for me, I could demonstrate that at the time they were not always catered for by the insurance industry as fully as they might have been. I stressed this point for all its worth in my renewed application and this time – and without any attempted bribe – I was successful: I was granted the permit, albeit only for 'arranging insurances for musicians'. I have to confess that I did not keep religiously to this limitation, otherwise I would not be here to tell the tale, having succumbed to inevitable starvation. Musicians do indeed have special insurance problems, one of the most serious being that they don't want to be bothered with insurance. Thus my official prospective circle of clients was not the easiest to do business with. Thankfully, nobody ever checked whether I strictly adhered to the conditions of my permit, and I believe this was the experience of other refugees too. Once we had received a permit to work freelance, the authorities ceased to be particularly worried about us as long as we did not change our occupation too drastically.

The residents of the boarding house where I stayed were almost exclusively refugees. As my very first effort in business, I started offering them insurance of their personal belongings, something which had not occurred to them insofar as they did not think they would have the necessary means for the premiums nor, for that matter, own anything worth stealing. However, helped by a fire that conveniently broke out on the upper floor of our boarding house – I swear I had nothing to do with it – I succeeded in effecting, I believe, eight policies on personal possessions for a sum of £100 each with a premium of 5/- (25p) a piece.

Clearly, at that time insurance companies did not insist on realistic minimum premiums as they rightly do today. My income from all these transactions totalled less than 50p gross – still, almost one day's living expenses. We may laugh about it now, but this is how many of us did start. I fear that transactions of this kind cannot have impressed the British world of commerce and can have done nothing towards persuading it of the value of refugees' business acumen. Hence we had some leeway to make up once we had got into our stride.

As I have mentioned, after some time, social and financial distinctions between refugees began to reappear. The interesting thing was that when everybody had begun to find his or her own level, it was in the majority of cases the same one they had occupied prior to emigration. Not that it was always easy to find out precisely what that had been. Some people used to boast about the prominent positions they or their families had held at home: the 'largest' this, the 'most important' that. But not infrequently those who did were grossly exaggerating – we called them 'Bernhardiners'.

It almost became the rule that the more a person moaned about his or her present lowly position as compared with that held previously, the less the complaint was justified and vice versa. Prime examples were some of the refugee ladies working as domestics. One of ours could not tell us often enough how demeaning she found her present work compared with what she had been used to in her family. In an unguarded moment, though, she let slip that her father had been a lorry driver, a most respectable occupation but hardly upper class. Her successor with us just did what she was supposed to do without ever complaining. After the war she received compensation for the expropriation of her late father's factory; he had been a millionaire many times over. Her starting wage with us had been 17/6d (87p) per week, which was the remuneration she had requested.

I know of cases where the wage was as low as 10/- (50p). Of course, one should not let oneself be misled by these figures. The cost of food, clothing and other amenities as well as rents was in proportion. The weekly rent for my first room, bed and breakfast, was £1.37. There were many shops selling shirts for 5/-, and suits for 50/- ('the 50/- tailors'). I remember admiring a friend who had undoubtedly 'arrived': he had had a suit made to measure by Austin Reed for £6. One of my clients owned an excellent Chinese restaurant in Wardour Street. If I wanted to take friends or clients out for a good Chinese meal I used to take him to one side: 'I'll pay 4/6d (22p) per head. You choose the menu. I'm relying on you for a slap-up meal.' I was never disappointed. (I recently came across the catering bill for my own wedding reception for about 50 people: it amounted to 30 guineas. But this is by the way.)

There were cases of people who in their homeland had not amounted to much (or who had been too young to ever prove themselves) but who became extraordinarily prominent and successful in emigration. Sometimes their grand ideas caused unease in the minds of their parents who had emigrated with them. One man I happen to know of will, I trust, forgive my mentioning him. I never met him myself, but a relative of mine was a close friend of his parents; his father was a scholarly man of modest means and he and his wife often expressed to my cousin their concern and misgivings about their son's high-flying attitude, in no way compatible with his station and expectations in life. He later became Lord Weidenfeld. Parents can be over-protective.

At the other end of the scale were some refugees

who had in fact occupied genuinely high positions in their homeland, but as emigrants could not make a go of things at all. I remember an elderly man (or what at that time we called elderly; he was probably in his fifties) whom, during my absence on war work, my firm had engaged in a very minor position purely as a favour to mutual friends. Eventually he gave in his notice – he had realised that he was completely useless and was very unhappy about it. After the war, he returned to Germany and was reinstated in his previous position – that of a *Reichsgerichtsrat*, a judicial member of the highest German court, equivalent to the House of Lords.

Our vulnerability was apt to create in us feelings of considerable ambivalence. This in turn had the effect of making us more critical of the British and their ways in respects other than those already mentioned. By now there were even some refugees who felt distinctly superior in many respects and took every opportunity to express that opinion – to us, their fellow refugees, at any rate. I have a suspicion that vis-à-vis Englishmen they wisely kept their mouths shut, because they, like most of us, wanted to become, as soon as possible, 'English' (or was it 'British' or even 'Scottish' or 'Welsh'? These distinctions caused many of us confusion, for on the Continent 'England' is usually equated with Great Britain.) However, critical or not, and being the assimilators that we were (and still are), most of us were only too willing to overlook the occasional weirdness of custom and to accept British ways to the full, especially as those we liked and admired predominated. In a way we were torn in two directions. It was undeniable that we found some conditions and customs difficult to comprehend and, in spite of our generally positive attitude, downright inferior to ours. Although I explore various aspects of this elsewhere in this book, let me mention a few here just to demonstrate.

Many of us had come from cities such as Berlin, Vienna and Munich, all outstanding cultural centres in their own right. And whilst Hitlerism had affected German culture to such an extent as to make it practically unrecognisable compared with what it had been, we remembered it as it had appeared to us in its heyday and could find little in our new country that was equivalent to it.

To a large extent the fault lay with us though it was, I think, forgivable. How could we, at that time, have any real understanding of British literature and its achievements? (The exception, incidentally, was Shakespeare: there were two outstanding, not translations but German re-creations, which had made his works very accessible to Germans. The original language, on the other hand, we found very difficult to understand). On some other points, we were undoubtedly right: British music, for instance, was distinctly lagging behind many Continental countries at the time.

On others we were again quite wrong: the theatre, for instance. We had considered German acting to be the best in the world. Austrian refugees, of course, thought the same of Austrian actors. We were convinced that, language difficulties notwithstanding, emigré actors would sweep the board. With very few exceptions, we were completely misguided. I remember the astonishment with which, after some years, I watched an old German film and, years later, a live performance in a German theatre. Compared to that in Britain and the USA, German acting sounded, more often than not, bombastic and unnatural. I have no experience of modern

German acting, but believe that the difference has meanwhile become less marked.

The same cannot be said of what the British were, and still are, pleased to call 'cabaret'. In Berlin, Vienna or Munich, 'cabaret' had meant two or three establishments producing, every evening, up-to-the-minute shows of the character, if not invariably the quality, of what in London represented a revolutionary new but apparently non-permanent development: the meteoric success of 'Beyond the Fringe'. Continental shows were to a large extent political and during the early Hitler period some of their stars and directors ended up in prison or even in concentration camps and the theatres were closed down on account of the critical political sketches shown. There was hardly anything of this kind in London at the time, and even today it is the exception. This can be clearly demonstrated by the sensationally successful post-war film 'Cabaret'. As a student, I was, like most young people, an avid follower of the Berlin cabaret scene, and I can truthfully say that I never, but never, saw anything even remotely like what calls itself 'cabaret' in that film. In this department we had, I believe, some reason to feel superior. I find it surprising that in a country as liberal and politically minded as Great Britain, 'real' cabaret has as yet failed to establish itself.

One institution which the overwhelming majority of us unreservedly admired was the British monarchy and all it implied, so different from what we had experienced since the First World War and, for that matter, from what the older generation had known of the German monarchy prior to it. Then, there had been the specific crime of *Majestätsbeleidigung*, *lèse-majesté*, with the courts sometimes imposing prison sentences on anybody who said or wrote anything nasty about the Kaiser or his family. This certainly could not be compared with the almost general acceptance, albeit not without criticism, of the British monarchy, nor the invariable custom, which we fully accepted – I suspect sometimes more readily than the British themselves – of playing the National Anthem at the beginning and/or the end of public performances and other events.

This, incidentally, is a nice example of how easily the customs of one country can be misinterpreted by the citizens of another. I remember a letter to my father during the inter-war years – written not by a refugee but by an American violinist who had been on a concert tour through England. He complained about the complete lack of musical understanding on the part of the British public: the audiences had no idea of what was being played. The only way to make it clear to them that a concert had come to an end was to play the National Anthem. Well, at least none of us refugees ever made that mistake.

English cooking gave rise to a lot of amused comment. 'Continental people live to eat, the British eat to live' was the often quoted chestnut. My own culinary skills amount to boiling eggs, brewing tea and preparing fast food as long as it can be kept in its sachet until ready to eat; hence I have no knowledge whatever of the subject and certainly no opinion on how much of the criticism was justified. But every person naturally likes his or her own national dishes and the way they are prepared. Even today I know Austrians, Czechs and Poles who love to visit what are basically not always very attractive restaurants solely because they serve their native dishes in the traditional manner. Curiously enough there seems to be, at the time of writing this, no restaurant in London serving genuine German food, possibly because the clientele would be too diverse. It might need four different sections: not only those for smokers and non-smokers, but also for former refugees and visitors from Germany!

However, when I first came to London, there was the well-known restaurant Schmidt in Charlotte Street. It had been there long before refugees had been ever thought of. Most of the waiters were, if memory serves me, Germans, and for all I know they and the management might have been ardent National Socialists. At any rate, they certainly were not over-polite to us but, interestingly, visiting Schmidts and eating German dishes was regarded by most of us as a great treat – once we could afford the prices. Eventually it closed its doors, but even today refugees of the older generation express a certain nostalgia at the mention of the name. It seems that it is not only love that 'goes through the stomach', if I may translate a German saying literally if clumsily.

Food preferences depend to a large extent on what you have been used to in childhood. Refugee children of school age, for instance, were quite partial to school meals whose typically English food, and the way it was prepared, were abhorred by their parents. I remember friends of ours telling us about taking their young children on a Continental holiday, where they indulged in all the delicacies on offer that were unavailable in England. On their way back, crossing the Channel on a British boat (at that time still the most common mode of travel), the children took one look at the menu in the dining salon and exclaimed gleefully, 'Goody goody, custard!' This was regarded by the older generation as a distinctly funny and at the same time highly regrettable aberration.

Something else we failed – and most of us still fail – to appreciate was the merit of early morning tea on an empty stomach: in my view a distinctly acquired taste, like haggis.

The English weather amused but did not particularly worry us. We found it funny that cricket and tennis, being so easily affected by the vagaries of the climate, were two of the most popular English sports. Yet no matter how often 'rain stopped play', the organisers somehow always managed to complete their programme in the end. This gave us an insight into the British genius for improvising and thereby overcoming a basically absurd situation.

On a more serious note, we were equally puzzled by the British first-past-the-post voting system. I felt that it was crazy by comparison with the utterly logical proportional representation system of the Weimar Republic, but I used to say it was proof that, as history showed, the most logical system is not always the one that works best in practice. I have to confess, though, that as regards the British voting system, I am no longer all that certain.

Another complete mystery to us was the question of when and when not to shake hands. In Germany you do (or at least did) it on every conceivable occasion; but in this country – when? Even today I still have the feeling that if an Englishman shakes my hand on taking his leave, he might be doing so in order to be polite and to show me that he is conversant with Continental ways. I myself have to remember the difference in local customs on every Continental holiday, in case I am regarded as rude.

On the other hand, I learned literally on the first day of my business career that the inviolate German rule of always keeping on the left of a lady or a senior person does not apply in this country. On that day my boss took me into the 'Room' at Lloyd's. In this very crowded market place he seemed to know a lot of people and kept turning and twisting in order to respond to greetings or have a word with a colleague. I had my work cut out to remain on his 'correct' side, circling him like a little dog. After about ten minutes of this he asked me with genuine concern: 'Are you deaf in one ear?' There is no more impressive way of learning what is and isn't customary in a foreign country, but I still take care to explain to female visitors from abroad why I walk near the pavement irrespective of which side I am on; they would otherwise think me bad-mannered.

Similarly, it took us some time to learn when and when not to call people by their first names. In Germany, during the early years, first-name-calling was highly unusual, partly no doubt because the German 'Du' and 'Sie' ('you' and 'thou'), contrary to English, where they are covered by the all-embracing 'you', denote differing degrees of intimacy and friendship. If I remember rightly, for the first three years my business partner and I – both refugees and on the closest terms of friendship – continued to address each other by our surnames prefaced by 'Herr'. And when we eventually got round to calling each other by our first names, this was by no means the final phase: we still continued with the 'Sie' and it took quite a while to reach the 'Du' stage.

Nor was it usual in Germany – except, I believe, on farms – to call employees by their first name. There is the charming story of the Berlin banker Carl Fürstenberg, famed for his wit as well as his wealth. After the revolution following the First World War, his coachman (cars were still very much the exception, horse-drawn vehicles demonstrating at that time a higher social and financial standing) came to him and said: 'Well, Mr Fürstenberg, we are now all equal. You can no longer address me as Joseph, but will have to call me Herr Müller.'

Fürstenberg replied, 'That's quite all right. But in future, please address me as Carl. There has to be a difference.'

When I started in business in England, the idea of calling any of my employees by their first name did not enter my head, until one day one of them asked me: 'Why don't you like me?'

'What do you mean? I do like you!'

'Then why don't you call me Tom?'

When, after retirement, at a very advanced age I accepted a job in a large firm of insurance brokers, most colleagues called me by my first name. But not all: interestingly, the younger they were, the more readily they did.

Another difficult question was at what stage to address a business connection by his first name. Of course, if you met for the first time at a business lunch, there was no doubt: it was all Nigel, John and Carl. The problem arose when you subsequently wrote them a business letter confirming what had been discussed. Would continuing with the first name sound over-familiar? Or, conversely, reverting to the last name too cold and distant? This is a specific refugee problem which does not seem to affect British-born people, to whom all this is far more natural than to us.

Another confusion – at the opposite end of the scale, as it were – arose from the fact that whilst in England only noblemen sign a letter with their surname without putting initials, in Germany signing with the surname only was (and I believe still is) the custom in practically any official or business letter. I remember several instances when British employees of mine expressed their sharp resentment at the presumption of German correspondents who signed in this way. However, at least initially, refugees in this country who did not yet know better committed the same *faux pas*. It sometimes took quite an effort to explain that there had been no intention on the writer's part to act above his station.

Linguistic difficulties abounded. Though I am devoting a special chapter to the funnier ones, there were plenty of everyday problems, some of which are worth mentioning here. In the early days, for instance, due to my initially poor English, I confined myself in restaurants to always ordering one of the two dishes whose names I could remember: roast beef or steak and kidney pudding. And I would like to put on record that I have never since succeeded, even at the best British restaurants, in ordering the latter dish equal in taste and quality – or at least so it seemed to me – to that served by the ordinary Lyons Tea-shop at sixpence ha'penny per generous portion.

Due to the vague way in which the English language expresses negative replies, it took us quite some time to realise that 'I don't think so', 'I'm afraid that' and similar expressions mean a definite 'no'. Many British people must have found us unnecessarily argumentative when, after receiving such an answer, we persisted in our endeavours, thinking the other person might change his mind. And sometimes we still take 'How are you?' literally, to the occasional discomfort of the questioner, and reply at length, forgetting the well-known admonition: 'Don't talk to me about your indigestion/ "How are you" is a greeting, not a question.'

Nor could we easily get used to the idea that 'half eight' means 8.30 and not, as it does far more logically in German, 7.30. Even today I tend to make doubly sure. And I was very unhappy when my boss, after a few weeks, said to me: 'You are no fool.' I did not realise that he had meant it as a compliment. Another misunderstanding: a young girl of my acquaintance was more than surprised that, when she was looking for a room, one prospective landlady refused to accept her because she had asked whether there was a 'Dusche' in the bathroom. The lady in question had understood 'douche' instead of what the girl had meant – a shower.

Many of us made fun of the fact that married couples used to call each other 'darling' even when quarrelling. Coming home from a visit to a 'genuinely British' couple who had been at loggerheads most of the evening but had still 'darlinged' one another all the way, we started to call each other 'darling' as well, purely as a joke. I have to say that after two days we got so used to it that we adopted that expression willy nilly for ever after.

Another word that created difficulties was the expression 'clever' which in German is not ever used in a disparaging sense. And I received another valuable lesson when a British grandmother whose grandsons I described as somewhat 'wild' (which in German means no more than boisterous) replied frostily, 'I shall thank you not to call my grandsons wild.' And finally, I shall not easily forget my depression when during my first weeks in London, I saw an American film starring Mae West and did not understand a word of what she was saying in her famous one-liners. (I don't understand much more today either, if I happen to come across one of her films.)

Very few of us went to language schools, relying instead on everyday experience. But I heard of a man who had an ingenious albeit most reprehensible method of scrounging free lessons: he regularly visited travel firms and enquired about world cruises, discussing them in every detail and endlessly wasting the staff's time. The language problem was one (but as I shall discuss in a different context, by no means the only) reason why we preferred the services of refugee doctors, dentists, solicitors and accountants permitted to practise to those of British-born professionals. This was despite the latter being equally – and in law and accountancy presumably better – qualified.

So much for the flavour of our first few years.

'Some of my best friends ...'

I

When, some time ago, I used this well-worn phrase in the company of friends, one of them, a Chinese antiques dealer living in London, replied, 'But *all* my best friends are Jews!' Coming from a non-Jew, a charming and heart-warming remark but, I think I am right in saying, rather the exception that proves the rule.

Being a refugee from Naziism with not a drop of non-Jewish blood in my veins, I am by definition both entitled and qualified to refer to my experiences on anti-Semitism. However, this does require some amplification, because my case is not quite typical in several respects. And though this book is in no way meant to be autobiographical, I feel it may be helpful if I mention some of my personal circumstances here.

The first is that I started life as a Christian. Shortly after my birth my siblings and I were baptised. Obviously not my own decision – I was what in German is so charmingly called a *Liegegoy**. I remained a Protestant until Hitler came to power, when I left the Christian church. The fact that I did not officially join any Jewish religious community made no difference to my position in Germany, which was purely based on race. The reason for my lack of religious initiative was the fact that, in our family, religion did not play any part whatever. I cannot remember a single occasion when it or my baptism were ever discussed. I was aware that I was of Jewish descent but it was not something that seemed to me of great

---

* Practically untranslatable; it means that I was made a Christian whilst as yet unable to stand on my own feet.

importance, even though I was, of course, conscious of the existence of anti-Semitism. At school I attended Christian religious instruction and was even confirmed. But I don't remember ever having entered a church on any other occasion except for the occasional attendance at a wedding or a funeral.

From the age of 15 until I had completed my schooling I attended the well-known German boarding school Salem, whose pupils were a mixture of different religions and races and came from every conceivable kind of background as far as their parents' social and financial standing was concerned. It made no difference. It took me longer than one term to realise that one of the older boys was the son of Prince Max of Baden, thus of royal blood. He was treated no differently from anyone else. The school's headmaster was Kurt Hahn, a Jew who subsequently became well-known in this country through having been in charge of the Duke of Edinburgh's education during his formative years.

The school's patron, in whose castle it was situated, was the above-mentioned Prince Max who, until 1918, had been the reigning sovereign of the Land Baden. At the very end of the First World War he had for a short time been made German Reichskanzler, being considered by the German High Command to be the most suitable sacrificial lamb to offer Germany's surrender to the Allies. Unsurprisingly – if I can be forgiven this mixing of metaphors – he had become and remained one of the radical right-wing parties' scapegoats ever since.

No religious instruction of any kind was given at Salem. Anti-Semitism and racism in any form were simply not an issue and therefore outside our experience during that period, irrespective of the individual pupil's family background. As it turned out, this was not the best preparation for real life.

My parents' decision to convert had undoubtedly not been motivated by religious considerations. At the time of my birth it was an accepted fact that conversion to Christianity offered in many cases a better chance of professional advancement, and for that reason quite a few German Jews took this step. Whether you were a Jew or not was, during that period, not a racial but a religious question, although the former could well play its part in the standing of converts in the eyes not of fellow- but of non-Jews. I am referring in the main to cases, by no means all that rare, in which a young aristocrat, usually from a family impoverished after World War I, married, for reasons best known to himself, a girl from a wealthy Jewish family. It has to be said that there were cases where the girl's parents, far from being distressed by her marrying out, were quite pleased with the match. It may, however, be assumed that in many cases the young wife was not fully accepted by some members of her husband's family.

With hindsight I naturally regret that my parents had me baptised. Religion or not, I would obviously prefer to have been an 'official' Jew from birth. But I doubt that it made a great deal of difference to my development, and I do not blame them in any way. Misguided or not, what motivated them was their children's welfare.

You occasionally hear about Jewish children or young people of Christian faith whose parents were foolish enough not to make them realise that they were members of the Jewish race, and who were deeply hurt when, after Hitler's arrival, they were suddenly ostracised by their friends and acquaintances both socially and professionally. This certainly was not so in my case. Nor, at the other end of the scale, did I feel in any way defensive, let alone inferior, vis-à-vis Jews just because some of them might look down on me as a converted Jew.

This had a specific reason: my father was a professional musician of world renown, and because of this, in my childhood, I regarded my family (however misguided this may have been) as superior to most others. Moreover, in the artistic world the Jewish question was of very little concern even then. Before my birth, my father had already been a professor at two State Academies of Music (in Roumania and Holland) and in the former country even an official court musician. I know of only one single anti-Semitic incident in his life, and that only because I read of it in his posthumously-published memoirs.

Originally he had studied music at the Vienna State Academy and as a young man had tried to become a member of the Vienna State Opera Orchestra. Its director was Josef Hellmesberger, a member of a well-known Austrian 'music family dynasty'. He had two violent dislikes: Jews and short-sighted people. My father happened to be both and Hellmesberger disposed of his application with the laconic file note 'Jew! Blind!' Shortly afterwards my father moved to Paris in order to complete his studies. If he had been accepted by the orchestra, he would have stayed in Vienna and probably remained a member of one of its very prestigious orchestras for quite some time. Hellmesberger's anti-Semitic reaction was therefore an undoubted blessing in disguise for him. Without it he would probably have missed his glittering career.

Purely as a curiosity, I would like to add what his rejection did for me. If my father had remained in Vienna, he would presumably have married an Austrian girl instead of my Dutch mother, whom he met during his professorship in Holland. This would have meant that, whilst there would no doubt have been children from that marriage, none of them would have been 'me'. Disregarding what happened later under Hitler to so many of us, there cannot be many Jews on whom one isolated anti-Semitic incident had a more profound influence than this one did on me, irrespective of my non-religious history. So there!

In a way I may be said to have been in a vacuum between two opposing worlds. So where did this leave me? It made no difference at Salem, but I attended that school only from the age of 15. Interestingly enough, looking back on the earlier period, I cannot remember having had a single non-Jewish friend. Basic Jewish characteristics obviously have nothing to do with the adherence to the Jewish religion. They go deeper. Understandably there existed an attraction between myself and those people who felt and acted the same as I did. As already indicated, none of my Jewish friends, some from quite orthodox homes, ever seemed to resent the fact that I was a converted Jew – a sign that this was by no means unusual at that time and certainly no cause for intolerance.

My personal experiences of anti-Semitism were so few that I can recall only one small incident, curiously enough during religious instruction for my Christian confirmation: the pupil sitting behind me chalked the word 'Jude' on the back of my coat and was severely rebuked by the pastor in charge of us. It made no particular impression on me. On the other hand, I vividly remember my older sister coming home from school one day in tears. A class-mate had called her a 'Jew girl'. I was at the time about ten years old. Surprisingly, in view of my general disinterest in these matters, this incident made me decide, before my parents could take any action, to persuade a few Jewish friends to appear with me in front of my sister's school in order to threaten the girl who had made that remark. This we did and it precipitated, inevitably, the end of my sister's career at that establishment, and not a moment too soon. What is interesting is that as a child I was neither on particularly close terms with my sister nor, as I have shown, particularly affected by Jewish matters. My reaction was therefore on the surface quite untypical and difficult to explain. Perhaps a deep-seated Jewish gut reaction overriding my conscious feelings?

II

As we all know, no country is, ever was or probably ever will be free from some form of anti-Semitism. As regards Germany, I think it is arguable that during the period following the 1914-1918 War, publicly-expressed (as opposed to latent) anti-Semitism was less rampant than many people are apt to believe today. And this despite the myth fostered by right-wing parties and readily believed by their followers that the German defeat had been due to the Jews (which led to the well-known Jewish question: 'Whose fault was it that Germany lost?' Answer: 'The Jews and the cyclists!' This inevitably resulted in the questioning reply: 'Why the cyclists?', to which our answer in turn was: 'Why the Jews?' I doubt, though, that it made many people stop and think).

Conditions changed somewhat in the 1920s, mainly because many people active in the financial sector were Jews. Or so at least it was alleged by the right-wing parties, and during the catastrophic inflation their activities were blamed as the main cause. But it is, I think, true to say that even at that time, anti-Semitism generally, outrages by extremists excepted, did not in fact express itself in as violent a manner as has often been suggested. Part of the explanation may have been the assimilation of German Jews who by appearance and manner were frequently not even identifiable as such. I shall have to say something about this later.

The degree of hostility expressed by anti-Semites may, as it were, partly lie in the eye of the beholder or, in this case, its victims. It has to be admitted that we Jews are particularly sensitive to anything that might indicate anti-Jewish-sounding sentiment, even where no offence is intended. This includes, for instance, our gut reaction to being called a Jew by a gentile.

I came across a striking illustration of this after World War II. It occurred on the occasion of one of the reunions arranged by many German towns and cities for their former Jewish citizens. The foremost idea in all these cases is to apologise for the atrocities inflicted by the Nazi regime. Accordingly, the organisers of these reunions bend over backwards to show their genuine contrition for the sins of their forebears. More often than not, Jewish emigrants who originally might have accepted the invitation to such an event with considerable hesitation and mistrust are won over by the feelings of regret so unreservedly displayed, and considerable goodwill is the result. To perpetuate this, some of the organisers make it their business to have a full report of the event prepared and sent to every participant as a permanent memento. Such documents often contain not only details of the meetings themselves but also personal accounts of the persecutions inflicted by the Nazi regime on some of the guests or their families, and the effect these had on them.

A few months after having attended one of these events (which had been particularly successful), I duly received such a report. Its author was a lady who during the event had not only gone to great lengths to do everything possible for the comfort of all the visitors, especially those handicapped by age or ill-health, but had also discussed their experiences, feelings, present attitudes and similar matters with many of them in some depth. She quoted a number of these interviews in detail, mentioning, with their permission, the interviewees by name. The result was not what she had so well-meaningly intended. In order to identify the category of persons concerned, she would write something like 'I talked to the Jewess Mrs Cohen' or 'the Jew Mr Levy'. I learned afterwards that some of the people concerned took great exception to being referred to in this way. And although I had not been one of the persons interviewed – my story was, happily, far too uninteresting for that – I have to admit that when I first read it, the expression jarred on me as well. On second thoughts it should not have done: if belonging to the Chosen People is a matter of pride to us, what is wrong with being called a Jew? It is true that the author could have used expressions like 'guest, participant, emigrant, former refugee, former co-resident' or whatever. But in the context of the talks, Jew and Jews was far more simple and to the point. It had not occurred to the lady that she might be causing offence.

Yet we are so used to the word 'Jew' being used disparagingly that our adverse reaction is an automatic reflex. And what is more, we take anything said against Jews as being personally directed against us. We ought to try and get over this, and perhaps one day we shall. But I would not advise my readers to hold their breath.

I experienced another example of our sensitivity when, some time ago, I read an article by the well-known political journalist Matthew Parris, who is not a Jew. It started with him relating a personal anecdote about anti-Semitism and then proceeded to describe a dinner party during which a lady sitting next to him had expressed herself in the strongest terms against 'those people', their attitude, wealth, the clandestine preferential treatment they gave to one another and so on. It seemed quite clear to the reader that she was referring to Jews. Whilst reading the piece, I became more and more irritated with her, mentally marshalling arguments to disprove her obviously erroneous beliefs.

Only quite at the end of the article did the author disclose, by means of a brilliant sleight of hand, that the lady had not been referring to Jews at all, but to homosexuals (Matthew Parris himself is an outed one). The effect on me was immediate: my wrath disappeared at a stroke. I have nothing whatsoever against homosexuals ('some of my best friends ...') and I find discrimination against them quite wrong. But I can discuss it rationally, without getting hot under the collar. Naturally, my – our – reaction to anti-Semitism is quite different, but this makes us psychologically more vulnerable than we would be if we were able to take a somewhat more detached view of what is, whether we like it or not, something we should have got used to by now.

There is, incidentally, a phenomenon which I regard as an interesting confirmation of this. A Jewish acquaintance of mine was once asked by a gentile British-born friend in genuine puzzlement: 'Why do you take every opportunity, openly and unasked, to emphasise the fact that you are a Jew?' Indeed, why do we? From pride? For the opposite reason that we don't want to give the impression of trying to hide something slightly shameful, especially if we happen to be not particularly Jewish-looking? From some sort of moral cowardice, because we want to prevent people we are talking to from making an anti-Semitic remark to which we would have to react? Or to forestall embarrassment? 'I know there are many anti-Semites about. In case you are one of them, make no mistake about who you are dealing with. Take it or leave it.' I have to admit that I don't know the answer, but it is almost certainly a combination of several of the factors just mentioned, and as such it should probably be regarded as an indication of subconscious tension and strain. I hasten to add, though, that under the Nazi regime, no Jew would have thought of tempting fate by drawing attention to himself in this way.

Today anti-Semitism falls into the more general category of racism. Our multicultural society has introduced so many more people against whom hatred can be directed that anti-Semitism has partly been replaced or, rather, become diluted by racism, which is dictated mostly by skin colour. (Hence the old saying: 'If God had not intended us to be racist, He would have made us all the same colour.') But anti-Semitism is still there, often subtle and hidden, and racism by colour is not something that ought to give us any grounds for satisfaction. Apart from the fact that the situation may well change again, racism, it goes without saying, must be condemned whoever it is directed against. But are we Jews quite free from it? Let us be frank: hands up those readers to whom the difference between themselves and, to be strictly politically correct let us call them 'more obvious other immigrants' is of absolutely no importance. Conversely, I have often wondered during sleepless nights what our attitude might have been if Hitler had not directed his wrath against the Jews but against, say, the Japanese. I can only hope that we all would have stood up against it. However, I digress.

German extremists, as we know, committed brutal murders and other crimes during the pre-Hitler-period, but they were mainly politically, not racially motivated. A typical example albeit in miniature, was the climate at the Berlin grammar school which I originally attended: my particular form consisted of almost 50 per cent Jews – an unusually high proportion for a state school – and as I remember it, whilst we were sharply divided, the enmity was not for racial or religious, but for political reasons. Jews being usually on the left, gentiles on the right, the almost automatic division between the two was somewhat coincidental. There were fights, of course, but curiously enough usually only between the two strongest boys of either faction (I am glad to say the Jewish boy usually won. Seventy years later I happened to meet him at a London charity concert and noticed with some amusement that my admiration for him had remained undiminished). The fights spread rarely, if ever, to the remainder of the pupils, who preferred the role of onlookers.

Nor, during my university years, can I remember any

personal overtly anti-Semitic experience. I have to say that my friends and I felt, no doubt often without any good reason, intellectually superior to most of our gentile colleagues. Even during the ascent of the Nazi party at the beginning of the 1930s, I personally experienced no anti-Semitism which could be called violent. Almost the opposite: during my time of post-university legal training as an unpaid civil servant (*Referendar*) in a small town east of Berlin, two Jewish colleagues and I decided one day to attend one of the frequent local Nazi rallies to find out first-hand what it was all about. Excitement during the meeting ran high and there was rapturous applause after almost every sentence uttered by the speakers. My friends and I did not, of course, participate, and after about half-an-hour this was noticed by one of the SA men acting as a steward. He came over, took a good look at us and said: 'Excuse me, are you Jewish?'

'Yes.'

'Then will you please leave the hall.' That was all. We made a dignified exit and nothing further happened.

It was the time-honoured custom for *Referendars* to be invited at least once during their term of training to the homes of the magistrates under whom they worked. Another 'non-violent' sign of the times: in our case – but not in that of our gentile colleagues – that custom was broken. We were merely amused by it. *Amtsrichter* – professional magistrates – in small German towns at that time usually represented one of the lowest forms of legal life.

It is often overlooked that initially the Nazis acted, if anything, more ferociously against their political opponents, not forgetting dissenters in their own party, than against the Jews. Anti-Semitism was, of course, one of the mainstays of their programme and was brought out on every conceivable occasion as an effective propaganda weapon; but Jews as such were not politically organised and therefore posed little threat initially. From the point of view of achieving and maintaining power they were not a priority. They could wait and remain on the backburner. As a matter of fact, the new rulers were initially even anxious to create a favourable opinion abroad and – as I happen to know first-hand – to show that they did not dismiss Jews wholesale, at least where such dismissals would be damaging to their cultural reputation outside Germany. My father had at that time a prominent position at the Berlin 'Hochschule für Musik', a state institution. The governing authorities went out of their way to try to keep him there. And in fact he stayed on for one year until it became obvious that the situation had become intolerable.

Thus the National-Socialists turned their full force on Jews only after they had successfully dealt with their political enemies. I remember a Nazi meeting during my student days in Heidelberg, open to all – the party was at that time still in opposition – at which the National-Socialist economic guru Gottfried Feder was the main speaker, expounding his theory of *raffendem und schaffendem Kapital* (grabbing and creating capital), thereby demonstrating that soundbites were well-tried propaganda tools even before the advent of TV and spin. Of course, there could be no speech by a National-Socialist that did not contain its full share of anti-Semitic remarks, but the prevailing sentiment on that occasion was less anti-Jewish than anti-government. There was some heckling, mainly from a girl student sitting in the front row who was well-known as an ardent Social-Democrat. The reason why she happened to be notorious for this was that she was the daughter of the president of the Reichsbank, Hjalmar Schacht, no less, as right-wing a politician and as 'Aryan' as they came, but at that time still a political anathema to the Nazis. One of the people on the platform recognised her and whispered her name to the speaker. There was no incitement to violence, but I cannot remember ever having heard more vituperative language than that used by the speaker against the young woman's father. Eventually she got up and left. I always remembered this scene when I saw a photo of Dr Schacht in the dock during the Nuremberg trials.

I have already mentioned that the average German Jew was by no means always easily distinguishable from the average German gentile. After the Nazis had achieved power, 'racial instruction lessons' had become obligatory in German schools. Cases of teachers calling a Jewish pupil to the front of the class in order to demonstrate a typically Aryan facial bone structure are well-documented. There was also the occasional case of a gentile businessman being urged for his own good to get rid of a Jewish partner. The only snag was that sometimes the partner thus approached happened to be the Jewish and the other, singled out for the attack, the gentile member of the board. And I recall in my early days as a refugee in London the prominent German gynaecologist Dr Loeser, a Jewish emigrant like myself, dining out on the fact that the official *Deutsche Ärzteblatt* (akin to, say, *The Lancet*) had quite recently published his photograph, taking up the whole of the front page, with the caption '*Das Gesicht des Deutschen Arztes*' ('The face of the [typical] German doctor'). The editor had evidently been misled by the fact that this man had, as a student, belonged to one of the few Jewish student organisations which supported duelling (*schlagende Verbindung*) and whose members proudly showed off their duelling scars – their *Schmisse*. This, together with a generally neutral appearance, had been sufficient for the paper to commit this embarrassing blunder. It shows how unreliable the distinction by outward appearance alone could be. I believe the newspaper cutting is now in the Wiener Library.

I myself had a similar experience. Jewish *Referendars* were, as unpaid civil servants, among the first to be dismissed on the 'Day of National Boycott' on March 31st 1933. At the time I was working in the public prosecutor's office. On the afternoon of the 30th, I was instructed by my boss (incidentally, an ardent anti-Nazi) to take a statement from an SA man held on remand for pickpocketing. Understandably the prisoner was on his best behaviour during the interview, mistakenly believing that I was of any importance whatever and therefore trying to get into my good books. When, at the end of the interrogation, I gathered up my papers, he remarked pleasantly: 'Isn't it wonderful that they'll be kicking out all the Jews tomorrow morning?'

The only reply I could think of was, 'I am a Jew and I'm still here.' The look of helpless consternation on his face was one of the few happy moments I remember experiencing during that traumatic time.

Anyway, I wasn't 'here' for long. The next morning I was unable to deliver my file, being prevented from entering my office altogether. I have always wondered what happened to that Nazi in view of his file having got lost. For all I know he may still be languishing on remand, making him the longest-serving prisoner in Germany. On the other hand, it is more likely that he became a Gauleiter somewhere.

The reality of German Jews and gentiles often being difficult to distinguish from one another was brought home to me again much later, in a different context. After the last war I visited Germany for the first time with a friend, a Jewish refugee like myself. One day we had arranged to meet at a restaurant, and I was sitting at a table watching the door so as to spot him right away. There was a constant stream of guests coming and going. Momentarily forgetting where I was, I mentally remarked to myself on seeing each new entrant: 'Ah, that's one of ours' (meaning a German refugee): then another, and another, till I suddenly realised with amused astonishment that I was not sitting in a London eating place catering mainly for refugees but in an original German establishment, and that the difference between German immigrants and 'genuine' Englishmen was usually far more marked than that between the average German Jew and German gentile

The day of the above-mentioned boycott was one of the landmarks signifying the beginning of the Nazis' relentless active anti-Semitic persecution. But even on that day I remember walking through the Berlin Westend, having just lost my job and thus with all the time in the world on my hands. I was amazed by the attitude of the thousands of 'nice'-looking Germans who crowded the streets. There was no obvious fanaticism, but rather an atmosphere of harmless fun, like a bank holiday on Hampstead Heath. They pointed out to each other and their children gleefully, but usually without sounding in the least malicious, the various insulting graffiti on Jewish shops and the SA men in front of them stopping the occasional defiant customer from entering (although most of the establishments had prudently remained closed anyway). It was then I realised that, for the time being, every layer of the German nation had become infected and there was nothing one could do about it in the foreseeable future.

This had not originally been the prevailing opinion. As a matter of fact, on January 30, 1933, the day Hitler came to power, I myself, a student greatly interested in politics and politically on the left, had experienced a certain sense of relief: 'At last. It had to come but it cannot last long. We can already see the light at the end of the tunnel. Let's get it over and done with as quickly as possible.' Many Jews felt the same and, tragically, did not change their minds in time. This was by no means due to stupidity on their part. There was no free press any more and rumours and all kinds of opinions were current. As a very minute observation, but possibly of interest in view of the dispute raging about the position and attitude of Pope Pius XII — about which I am in no way qualified to pass any opinion — it is worth mentioning that during his stay in Germany as *Nuncio Pacelli*, I remember his name being mentioned by us with a certain amount of hope and reassurance, a light in the darkness that surrounded us. I cannot recall why and I don't suppose there was any justification for it (we grasped at straws), but there may have been some glimmer of hope that he, as the representative of the Catholic Church, might somehow be instrumental in moderating the severity of our persecution; otherwise the idea would probably not have come up. At any rate, it was apparently without foundation.

Even the most experienced Jews were apt to assess

the situation wrongly. For me, the most memorable example of misjudgement will always remain that of Georg Bernhard, Editor-in-chief of the *Vossische Zeitung* (a paper comparable in standing to, say, *The Guardian*) who was also a Member of Parliament and a lecturer at the Berlin *Handelshochschule* (School of Economics). With all these means of direct information at his disposal, there could have been nobody better qualified than he to give an expert opinion. Our families were close friends and we were having a meal together at a Berlin restaurant – as it happened after my father's last public appearance on a Berlin concert platform (which incidentally brought him a mention in the well-known political novel *The Family Oppermann* by Lion Feuchtwanger. Unfortunately it was somewhat negative in context: the heroine of the novel on being invited by a friend to go to that concert, declined because she did not find it sufficiently interesting).

Suddenly, the news of the Reichstag fire came through on the radio. On hearing it, Georg Bernhard uttered his considered opinion, the most ill-judged seven words I ever expect to hear: 'This is the end of the Nazis!' We were all duly impressed and relieved. An outstanding expert like Georg Bernhard could not possibly be wrong. The rest, as they say, is history.

Gentiles were often equally naïve. One of them, the undoubted king of musical Berlin, Wilhelm Furtwängler (incidentally the conductor of the above-mentioned concert on the evening of the Reichstag fire), had several Jewish players in his Berlin Philharmonic Orchestra, including its leader as well as the head of the cello section. He did his utmost to keep them in the orchestra. I have a letter from him to my father in which he complained, when they eventually resigned, that he was being deserted by them and thus frustrated in his endeavours to keep German music in the high standing and reputation it possessed at the time. The idea that two Jews were hardly going to be of much use to him in this task, even if they had wished to stay, did not occur to him. He was a German nationalist – and why shouldn't he be? – but certainly anything but an anti-Semite. I have read in a biography about him that the BBC took no notice of any letter from Furtwängler recommending a refugee for a job: his opinion was bound to be favourable, regardless of real merit, and therefore of no value.

III

When, in 1934, I arrived in England, I did not expect any anti-Semitism nor did I personally experience any. Surprisingly, with hindsight, the Mosley movement made very little impact on my friends and myself. We did not even consider the possibility of the German example – the rise of Fascism from utter obscurity – being repeated in our new country. On the other hand, during those early days there was, in some British circles, an almost breathtaking lack of understanding of the reasons that had forced us to leave Germany. As far as the man in the street was concerned, I could discern little anti-Hun feeling at that time, nor more than occasionally any outright condemnation of the German treatment of Jews. On the contrary, I remember not one but two occasions on which someone expressed to me the hope that England and Germany would march together against the French one day soon!

But while this may be seen as harmless idiocy, it was

soon after I had started my training with a well-known firm of Lloyd's brokers that I became greatly disillusioned with British feelings towards Jews in general, or at least in the field of Insurance, Lloyd's in particular. The latter, to put it very mildly, were not over-enamoured with Jews. This has changed somewhat since, but I am not all that sure by how much: when at the end of the 1980s the well-known Lloyd's scandals occurred, bringing that institution to the brink of destruction and costing its members billions, completely ruining many and even driving a few to suicide, everybody was looking for scapegoats. A great many people, in particular underwriters, managing and members' agents, were accused of gross incompetence, all kinds of misdeeds and – almost certainly wrongly – even fraud. I am pleased to say that I cannot recall a single Jew being named among those held responsible. Clearly, no member of the Jewish race had achieved a prominent position in Lloyd's or else he would have been the first to be singled out. This was one of the very few cases in which the result of anti-Semitism turned out to be a blessing, however much in disguise.

At any rate, in the 1930s, anti-Semitism in the insurance industry was rife, in part no doubt due to a sensational case that had been headline news shortly before my arrival. A prominent Jewish claims adjuster who, clearly bucking the trend, had enjoyed the fullest confidence of leading insurance companies including Lloyd's, was exposed as a criminal swindler who had been 'assessing' a number of claims in collusion with the claimants and, I was told by colleagues, had even been a party to fires being started by the insured themselves. He received a substantial prison sentence, but the damage had been done: 'There you have it again, you just cannot trust a Jew'.*

I was shocked, but worse was to come. I found that the majority of Lloyd's syndicates transacting motor insurance were loath to accept Jewish business, some barring it absolutely. The official reason given was that their mental make-up made Jews generally bad drivers – an obviously inane opinion, usually only held by some of their spouses. But in fact, this was not only the view at Lloyd's. There was at least one large international insurance company, the Zurich, whose UK subsidiary generally did not discriminate against Jews at all, except for one strict rule of whose justification it was wholly convinced: it never knowingly accepted Jewish motor insurance business. For an insurance broker like myself, this was doubly awkward, because the Zurich had at that time a special scheme by which they insured Ford cars at a cheaper rate than any other company in the market. I am sure that they had to accept Jewish cases under this general agreement, but apart from that they would not entertain any such cases offered by independent brokers.

Until, that is, one day something peculiar happened. One of my Jewish clients, a refugee and a particularly nice young chap, a student at a rabbinical college, had acquired a Ford and asked me to insure it with the Zu-

---

* This was certainly not shared by the judiciary. For when this man, after completing his sentence, resumed his profession as a claims assessor (acting, of course, only for the insured who had to make a claim, not the insurers), one of his prospective clients, on discovering his history, cancelled the contract. The assessor sued and won. The court held that he had, through his prison sentence, paid his debt to society and his track record was no longer relevant. Personally, I disagree with this decision, but it certainly shows a welcome lack of anti-Jewish sentiment.

rich. 'No can do,' I replied, explaining the circumstances and suggesting he should cover the car directly under their special scheme where it would most probably slip through unnoticed.

'No way,' said he and took his proposal personally to the company's head office, explaining that he was a Jew and asking to be insured. Two hours later he returned to my office, triumphantly waving a cover note: 'No trouble at all!' Admittedly, it may have helped that he looked anything but Jewish – by appearance he could have passed for a Hitler Youth – but he had deliberately drawn the company's attention to his race and dared them to refuse him. I never found out what precisely had happened – the company would not be drawn – and they did not change their general attitude until much later. I feel this is an interesting example of a man taking the bull by the horns to defeat prejudice. At first glance it lends fuel to the accusation not infrequently levelled against us by English Jews that if we had not been so eager to assimilate but had stood our ground, the whole German tragedy would have been avoided. There can be no doubt whatsoever that this assessment is completely wrong. The two situations are in no way comparable, as our accusers would have quickly realised had they been Jews in Germany at that time.

A refugee friend of mine had a different method of nailing anti-Semites. From her outward appearance you would not have guessed that she was Jewish, hence from time to time people unsuspectingly expressed to her adverse criticism of the character and behaviour of Jews. In these cases she used to reply compassionately: 'I'm sure you are quite right. You must have had some terrible experiences with them. Tell me – what were they?' Needless to say, the speakers would normally be thoroughly nonplussed, especially when she disclosed the fact that she was Jewish herself. However, I have no knowledge of instances where those people changed their opinions as a result.

Prejudice in the insurance industry against Jews generally and refugees in particular was not restricted to motor insurance; it often also turned up in other types of private insurance, in particular that of personal belongings. It is an indisputable fact that people living in certain districts are particularly high burglary risks. Many of the residents in these districts were and still are German or Austrian Jewish refugees. It is a fact of life that many people in this category possess more valuables than gentiles in the same income bracket. There are several reasons for this. On the one hand, Jews in many countries had been prevented for centuries from owning land and therefore had to look for other investments; on the other, being frequently uncertain whether or not pressing circumstances might necessitate a move at the shortest possible notice, they preferred possessions that were small in size compared to their value and easily transportable – eg jewellery. So, for precisely the same reasons, do burglars.

This understandably pertained doubly to refugees from Germany who frequently had deliberately converted as many of their assets as possible into valuables prior to emigration, thereby making themselves disproportionately high burglary risks. But as a matter of fact, and not only in the insurance industry, it often went deeper than that: there was a general mistrust of foreign-born residents in Britain (as compared to foreigners living in their own native country). I deal with this question in a different context in this book.

Anti-Semitism can be deliberate (of the 'Church nearby'-type in former advertisements for hotels which did not welcome Jews), or it can be quite unconscious. I think that refugees mainly encountered the latter. For instance, in the course of my professional work I looked after the insurances of a number of small Jewish organisations for whose staff I sometimes arranged pension schemes with one particular insurance company which offered, at that time, the most favourable terms. On one occasion I ventured to remark to a representative of that firm that I had placed three such schemes with his company during the last few months. I expected a few well-chosen words of appreciation for offering them this sought-after business. Instead, what I got was an undoubtedly well-meant, 'Oh that's quite all right. Please don't worry about it.' I am sure the man who gave me this answer intended no rudeness, nor had any wish to hurt my feelings. He did not have the slightest inkling how utterly offensive he was being. In another case a friend of mine had a dispute with a fellow refugee and consulted the Citizens Advice Bureau. Having heard the story, the 'expert' nodded sagely and remarked, 'So it's Jew against Jew.' I was never told by my friend whether or not the quality of the 'advice' improved after that. However, it is well-known that the CAB has meanwhile become highly professional.

But conscious discrimination against Jews is not necessarily motivated by anti-Semitism either. It happened to me: I had put down my son's name for a well-known public school. He sat the entrance exam but was not accepted. The headmaster asked me to come and see him. He apologised: 'Actually your son passed, but, being a Christian foundation, we have to restrict our intake of Jewish boys. Unfortunately there were other Jewish children better than him. I am sorry, we would like to have him. I suggest you let him sit again next time.' I don't know whether I did the right thing, but I swallowed my pride and agreed – and the same happened again. I believe that today's legislation against racial discrimination would prevent a similar occurrence. But I am sure that at the time the school would have considered it an injustice if steps had been taken against it.

The story has an intriguing sequel. 'I'll show you,' I thought. As already mentioned, I had been a pupil of the German boarding school Salem whose Jewish headmaster, Kurt Hahn, due to his fearlessly outspoken views, had for some time been imprisoned by the Nazi government. He had subsequently emigrated to Scotland and founded the school Gordonstoun. It had rocketed to fame because one of its former pupils, Prince Philip, had just married the future Queen of England. Headmasters are always flattered when old boys place their children with their former school, and Kurt Hahn accepted my son most readily. But then a snag arose. Hahn had converted in England and become a member of the Church of England. My wife expressed strong scepticism about his reasons and insisted that I ask him why he had done it – not an easy thing to do under any circumstances, but particularly not with a man of the calibre of Kurt Hahn, whose commanding influence on Prince Philip's thinking could be detected by cognoscenti in the latter's speeches for quite a number of years.

However, I did as I was told and received a frank answer: 'I did it from conviction. I neither sought nor derived any advantage from it, but I consider that communism can only be fought on a Christian basis.' This was a fully satisfactory answer for any former pupil of Kurt Hahn who had been able to observe his moral fibre, which was beyond any doubt whatsoever. It is certainly difficult to see in what material way he could possibly have profited: not only had Prince Philip been a pupil at his school while Kurt Hahn had still been a Jew, but the reason the Nazis had released him from prison had been the intervention of influential British friends on his behalf. Clearly his Jewish religion had not affected them adversely. Thus nobody could question his motives when the subject of his conversion happened to be discussed, as it was quite frequently at the time. Unless you consider it significant that, as became known many years later, the British authorities had him watched as a potential German spy during the last war – a wholly ludicrous assumption and waste of public money.

.The intention of this book is to apply my personal experience to that of my fellow refugees as a group. I have to confess that I cannot contribute a great deal to the question of anti-Semitism in England beyond what I have already written. One of the reasons could be that, due to my religious 'non-history', I never found my way towards membership of a Synagogue. But I rather doubt it. Whatever the orthodox view, it is race rather than religious observance which these days is the deciding factor in the question of whether you consider yourself a Jew and are one in the eyes of the Jewish and non-Jewish communities. I realise the difference in attitude between English and German Jews, but I venture to doubt that whatever anti-Semitism British Jews experience has very much to do with religion either. The only time I heard the Jewish religion discussed by gentiles was while I was working in a factory during the Second World War. Many of my fellow workers were gentiles who happened to have been brought up in or near London's East End. They recalled the fact that several of them had been used by orthodox Jews as 'Schabbes Goys', ie non-Jews carrying out activities such as lighting fires etc, forbidden to Jews on a Sabbath. There was never any hostile comment, just a sense of tolerant amusement at some of the quaint Jewish customs that enabled gentiles to make an honest penny from something that could not really be called 'work'.

Whether I am the exception or just being particularly unobservant, I can, apart from the instances mentioned in this chapter, hardly remember having encountered any overt or subconscious anti-Semitism in my private or business life. Nor did I perceive any particular reluctance on the part of British-born gentile job applicants to join a firm run by Jewish immigrants except on one occasion: a man to whom I had offered a job refused it on the grounds that he felt that, if he were to be by any chance in a dispute with one of my Jewish employees, he would always be at the losing end, since I would automatically side with the other man. I was unable to disabuse him of this entirely misguided opinion. On reflection, however, I am beginning to wonder whether there might not have been a grain of truth in his opinion and I would subconsciously have acted as he suspected. On the other hand, his refusal may just have been a diplomatic way of saying 'no' to a refugee firm.

But taken all in all, anti-Semitism by the British people was not one of our most pressing issues. Instead it was the fact that we were not British-born, but aliens. This was by far the more dominant factor, overshadowing and encapsulating, as it were, any anti-Semitic problems. (After all, if you were a Hitler refugee, you were by definition practically certain to be Jewish.) I doubt that the very few gentiles who emigrated from Germany on account of their previous political activities or simply from moral conviction were regarded by the bulk of the British population in a different way from us.

In either case the real question for those of us who wanted to stay was when, if ever, were we going to be accepted as fully-fledged Britishers? And that is what most of this book is about.

Language, humour, names and all that

I

You will recognise the German Jewish refugee not only, as I have already noted with regret, by his accent, but also by certain mannerisms of speech. For instance, if you hear someone saying repeatedly 'Thank you so much', you can assume fairly safely that he was originally German. For some reason this particular phrase has impressed us deeply, probably because it is so entirely different from what is correct usage in German and is therefore regarded by us as particularly 'good English'. On the other hand, if someone asks us whether we would like, say, a second helping of something, and we would, we usually cannot bring ourselves to say a simple 'Thank you', because in German this can mean 'No'. And if the question happens to concern a liquid refreshment and we are asked, 'Would you like some more tea?', ten to one you won't hear us reply, 'Yes please, but only a drop'; it comes out as 'but only a bit' ('ein bißchen', German for 'a little').

Generally, on the other hand, we like to anglicise even where this is unnecessary. For instance, the well-known pianist Natalia Karpf once told me that while British people would pronounce her first name correctly as in 'Natalia', refugees would invariably persist in calling her 'Natalee'. Sometimes we take on the accent of that part of the country where we happen to live. I was amused by a client of mine, a factory owner who spoke English with a Berlin accent you could have cut with a knife, but who would invariably pronounce the word 'girl' as 'gel', something that was correct in the local dialect but sounded extremely strange when said by him. And generally there are a number of words whose correct pronunciation we find it very difficult to ascertain, partly because sometimes the natives differ themselves: 'dandelion', 'awry', 'subsidence' (this, incidentally, not even the BBC knows). Some can't pronounce the word 'misled' properly. And an acquaintance of mine was puzzled for a long time about what a 'milk pond' was (what was meant was 'mill pond'). Correct pronunciation is the main stumbling block. It reminds me of the story of the refugee who saw the newspaper headline of a review: 'Hamlet pronounced success.' This was the moment when he realised that he would never master the secrets of English pronunciation and started to learn Chinese instead.

You will sometimes recognise newly arrived refugees by their basically-correct but rather old-fashioned language — 'descend', 'impose', 'implement' and so on. There was the 15-year-old refugee girl befriended by a British family who quarrelled with the son of her hosts and said to him haughtily, 'I shall have no more intercourse with you.' My own father, before his emigration, once wrote to a London friend asking him to contact me. He meant to say that I was staying at the same boarding house as a mutual acquaintance but it came out as 'My son Carl is living with Mr X.' It may have been my imagination, but I had the distinct impression of encountering some raised eyebrows next time I met my father's friend.

Generally, people are apt to give others' choice of words an unexpected sexual connotation. I shall not easily forget my embarrassed disappointment when, as a trainee with a firm of Lloyd's brokers, I showed my departmental manager a letter from the mother of a violinist, a child prodigy of some fame, whose violin I was being asked to insure. It was one of my first pieces of business and I was quite proud to have gained such a prominent client. But instead of words of encouragement I just received helpless laughter. The boy's mother, describing the violin, had written, 'My son has a very big instrument ...' More serious, perhaps, was the story of a young girl who one afternoon visited the cinema by herself and had the ill-luck to find herself sitting next to an amorous neighbour who started fondling her knee. Horrified, she exclaimed: 'Go on, go on!' I have no idea how the episode ended.

One divorced lady once complained bitterly about her husband who had suddenly left her after a 'ravenous marriage'. There is the story of another girl who, when asked by her office colleagues whether she had enjoyed a short leave of absence due to a family bereavement, replied, 'Surely not, as you can imagine: I was on passionate leave'. My little son was sorely puzzled when, on his 6th birthday, an old lady wished him 'many happy regrets'. This was similar to the refugee guest who, on taking leave from his hosts, said, 'Thank you very much for your hostility'.

Two stories which I am assured are true: one tells of a refugee who wanted to find a tea shop where he could have a cup of tea. He puzzled a passer-by with the question: 'Are there any Lyons around here?' The other is that of a Hungarian immigrant who wanted to ask the way from a gentleman who, try as he might, was quite unable to understand what was wanted of him. Being of a kind disposition, he eventually assumed that the man, who was pretty shabbily dressed, was begging and asked him, 'Are you hungry?' Highly pleased at having at last been able to get through, the Hungarian exclaimed, 'Yes,

yes, I am!' 'Come with me,' the stranger said and took him to a restaurant where he ordered a sumptuous meal for him. 'Are you still hungry?' he asked at the end.

'Yes, I am!' It apparently took some time for the crossed lines to be disentangled.

Sometimes misunderstandings can be more embarrassing. There was a Jewish refugee couple, sincerely welcomed by the inhabitants of a small village. At Christmas they were invited to midnight carols and it was suggested to them that they should choose a hymn celebrating Christmas, something, I have to confess, that was by no means difficult for many German Jews. They knew precisely how to oblige their hosts with the right song: the German 'O Tannenbaum, o Tannenbaum, wie grün sind deine Blätter.' ('Oh Christmas tree, oh Christmas tree, how green are your leaves.') There was, as it turned out, just one snag, which must have had a somewhat dampening effect on the Christmas spirit: the tune of that song is the very same one performed enthusiastically by the British Labour Party at every meeting: 'The Red Flag'. Incidentally, in German there are a few less respectful versions of 'O Tannenbaum' and consequently no original refugee has ever been able to take 'The Red Flag' seriously after having heard it sung in Great Britain – once he had recovered from his surprise, that is.

Staying with the church, two eight-year-old boys, twins, who had come over with a Kindertransport, were fostered by a very nice couple in a village and received many small kindnesses and gifts from other villagers. Their foster parents were devout Christians who attended church every Sunday. So as not to leave the children unsupervised, they took them along. When the collecting plate went round and people dropped their pennies into it, the children, who had not understood a word of the service, came with compelling logic to the conclusion that these too were presents intended for them. So when the plate reached them, they tried to grab all the money in it. This, I gather, was their first and last church attendance. One can only hope that no-one in the congregation found themselves convinced of what they had doubtless often been told about the avarice of Jews.

The everyday matters of life were (and sometimes still are) equally full of pitfalls for us. What refugee in his early days could tell the difference between jam and marmalade, ham and bacon? Why did the British eat grass sandwiches (mustard and cress)? How could a father know that a kite he wanted to buy for his son's birthday was not called a 'dragon' in English as it is in German? The coal merchant who was asked by the lady of the house to deliver his load 'into my back passage' may have received the wrong impression of his customer – as may the firm with whom a refugee lady tried to discuss the repair of her 'shits'. When this had been cleared up, it turned out that the company in question were actually watch repairers whom the lady had mixed up with 'Wäsche' (linen) restorers. And the British family who had provided a home for a refugee boy considered him to be of subnormal intelligence when he simply could not understand why they wanted him to buy vinegar – 'Vinegar of what?' 'Just vinegar.' – until it turned out that what he had understood was 'weniger', which means 'less' in German.

One Austrian lady went into several kitchen shops trying to buy a 'creator'. She was unable to understand why the British did not know of the existence of such an everyday implement. Eventually the riddle was solved.

What she had wanted to buy was a ladle, which in her home country is called a 'Schoepfer'. But the German dictionary she consulted was not aware of this particular meaning of the word. It had only the customary translation of 'Schoepfer': the 'creator' of the world – God. Other difficulties were more easily cleared up. One lady had forgotten the word for 'chicken', but was able to make herself correctly understood by describing it as 'the bird who lays eggs'. Another asked for 'dukes' eggs'. Sometimes mistakes can be immediately deciphered by fellow refugees, like that of the man who told his friend that he had had his 'blind gut' removed – the literal German translation of appendix.

On occasions, of course, the boot is on the other foot and it is the British who make linguistic bloomers in German – as did a man I know who visited a German town. Being a collector of toy pistols, he went into a shop first thing and bought two of the German version. Returning to his hotel, he was anxious to try them out without delay but in order not to disturb his neighbours, he decided to muffle the sounds with his bed cover. The inevitable result was, of course, massive scorching. Being an honest man, he went down to reception and reported the mishap to the shocked consternation of the receptionist at the desk: 'Ich habe in mein Bett geschossen'.

II

Understandably, refugee jokes are in the main about language difficulties, changes of name and similar matters. The point of these tales is that the perpetrator is not supposed to realise that he is saying or doing anything peculiar. In this way, he is apt to become an involuntary figure of fun, possibly even of pity. However, as far as refugee – or for that matter most Jewish – jokes are concerned, I maintain that this is usually far from true. I feel certain that most of these stories, and in particular those concerning our linguistic failings, were either deliberately invented by refugees themselves or, as far as they were involuntarily perpetrated, gleefully spread by them. This was one of the ways in which we were able to try and come to terms with some of the difficulties of our situation. And how else could these stories have been put about? Certainly not via non-German speaking people, who would not even be able to see the point of most of them.

Whether I am right or not, we refugees were (and are, as I have already shown) certainly not alone in committing linguistic boobs. A nation whose Government spokesman, on being asked in the House of Commons about the Prime Minister's plans for the rest of the day, can reply, 'This afternoon Mrs Thatcher is making herself available to Mr Gorbachev' certainly does not have the right to laugh 'at', only 'with' us.

When I first considered whether I should devote a chapter of this book to refugee jokes, I wondered whether it might be a waste of time. Refugees have heard and retold them so often that they are not just 'old' but 'ancient' hat. Was there really any point in dusting them off yet again? However, on reflection I realised that 60 to 70 years have passed since the 1930s and early 1940s, ie not just one but almost two generations. As you get older you tend to overlook the passing of time. I realised this only too clearly when I recently met someone who quite obviously was not yet in his fifties, and asked him unthinkingly what he had been doing during the war, completely overlooking the fact that he had not yet been born at that time. This sort of thing is probably one of the reasons why younger people so often no longer take us oldies seriously. On the other hand, stories that are 65 years old plus may be new for many people today. Anyway, don't we always say that the old jokes are the best? Of course, my fund of stories is limited and consequently I wrote a letter to *AJR Information*, the official German Jewish refugee paper, asking readers for help. I was overwhelmed with replies from many kind people whose names I have mentioned (I hope all of them) in my acknowledgements at the beginning of this book. It was interesting to note, incidentally, that amongst many others, one or two stories were quoted in almost every reply.

Language jokes, though, often present yet another difficulty: most of them are plays on words which can be appreciated only by people who speak the foreign language in question, in our case German. Non-German speaking people – and I am hoping that this book will be of interest to some of them too – will not understand them spontaneously. Having to explain a joke is, as we all know, giving it the kiss of death. Nevertheless, I decided that explanations, where necessary for understanding, were the lesser of two evils. I first considered relegating them to footnotes so that German-speaking readers would not have to bother looking at them, but I found this made reading them far less convenient. I hope my German-speaking readers will bear with me. So here goes, with a few examples. It is not always possible to be certain about their 'pedigree'; a few may not even have originated with refugees at all. But if they didn't, they should have done.

To start with a few chestnuts (I forbear to repeat the daddy of them all, ascribed, I believe, to the first German post-war President: 'Equal goes it loose', a literal translation from the German for 'It [whatever the event was] will start any minute'):

- On a crowded bus a refugee couple get separated, the wife finding a seat on the lower, the husband on the upper deck. When the conductor comes to collect the fare, the wife, who has no money on her, tries to indicate that her husband will settle it. But the way she puts it is liable to be misunderstood: 'The Lord is above, he will pay'.

- A customer in a bakery observes another woman, somewhat heavily made-up, selecting a cake which she considers would be a suitable purchase for her too. She turns to the shopkeeper with the words: 'Can I become a tart like this?' (the only German meaning of tart – 'Torte'– is 'cake'. 'Bekommen' in German means 'get'). There are several versions of this joke, the best one, to my knowledge, with the greengrocer replying: 'Too late, my dear, too late.' And there is another story (which I only mention for the sake of completeness, for every refugee knows it) with the same play on words. A woman at a greengrocers, on being told the price of cauliflower, indignantly exclaims: 'Such much? I can become a cauliflower round the corner for sixpence. Behold it.' ('Behalten' is 'to keep' in German.)

- A refugee complaining to his boarding-house proprietor: 'Expensive landlady! There is a train in my room and the ceiling is too short. If things don't improve, I shall have no election but to undress.' (All words have double meanings. 'Expensive' = the German 'teuer'= 'dear'; the word for 'train' can also mean 'draught'; 'ceiling' = the German 'Decke', which can also mean blanket; 'election = 'Wahl' which in German also means 'choice'; and 'undress' in German is 'ausziehen', which can also mean 'move'.) I should perhaps add that in pre-war days the antiquated British heating and ventilation systems were a constant wonder to foreigners. Possibly on account of the prevalence of open fireplaces, draughty rooms were one of the main reasons for complaints by people arriving from abroad, whereas the British did not seem to mind them at all. There is no precise English expression for the all-embracing German word 'gemütlich' – 'comfortable' 'cosy' etc do not entirely fit. Someone suggested 'draughty' as the most suitable equivalent.

- Another refugee has rented a room in a private flat. Late at night the telephone rings. The landlord is out, so the tenant answers it but cannot understand what is being said. In his frustration he shouts, 'Vy must you rink now? It is mitnight and I am only a ghost here' (Confusion with 'guest'). He was no doubt the same man whose rent included 'lightning'.

- Probably the same refugee again, alone in the flat, this time during the day, answers the door to the gas man who says, 'I've come to see the meter.'
'I am the Mieter. Vat do you vant?' ('Mieter', pronounced 'meeter' in German, means 'tenant').
An extended version is the gas man replying, 'No, you are not', to which the tenant answers 'Yes, but I am

the undermieter (subtenant)'

- A tourist arriving in Hawaii asks a stranger, who happens to be probably the only refugee who originally made it to Hawaii: 'Excuse me, can you tell me, do you pronounce this place Hawaii or Havaii?'
'Havaii.'
'I see, thank you very much!'
'You're velcome.'

- A woman goes into a chemist shop wanting to buy paper. 'Paper? I am afraid we don't sell paper.'
'Yes, you do, it is the paper – ah – ah – for the smallest room.'
'Oh, you mean toilet paper?'
'Yes.'
The transaction having been satisfactorily completed, the chemist asks 'Is there anything else you would like?'
'Yes, some soap, please.'
'Toilet soap?'
'No, for the face.'
This, presumably, is not a true story, and brings me to the large number of jokes and anecdotes that have entered refugee lore.

- In the early days, marriages between female refugees and Englishmen were a rarity and, it must be admitted, sometimes probably marriages of convenience from the lady's point of view. In one such case the bride, on being asked at the marriage ceremony to repeat 'I shall obey my lawful husband', is said to have repeated it in the best Freudian tradition as 'I shall enjoy my awful husband'. Hopefully she was not the same lady about whom it was said later, 'Her marriage has not been consumed'.

- During the early years of the last war the official bulletins unfortunately had to report a string of disasters for the British. Two refugees are discussing the situation: 'Can you understand these reports?'
'Oh yes, quite well. Only one thing puzzles me: who is this General Wit-h-Drawal who is being mentioned so frequently?'

- A written invitation ends with the words 'Don't dress as we shall be intimate.' (A literal translation with a nice double entendre. In Germany, in the olden days, 'to dress' meant to dress formally. The word 'intim' had no sexual connotation. 'Im intimen Kreise' simply meant 'amongst good friends', 'informal dress'.)

- On a wedding invitation the recipient, a refugee, is puzzled by the foot note 'RSVP' and asks a friend what he thinks it means. 'Quite simple: Remember se veddink present.'

- An immigrant, being asked at the customs whether his luggage contains any pornographic material, replies: 'No. I don't even possess a pornograph.'

- A recently arrived refugee at a bus stop: 'I know myself not out. Must I stand snake?' (Literal translation of the German grammatical structure, plus that in German to 'stand snake' means 'to queue'. 'Schlange' means 'snake', hence 'Schlangestehen' in German.)

- Board meeting of a company whose directors are all refugees. The firm's accountant asks: 'Who is chairman?'

'We all are, but we are naturalised British.' (The way refugees mispronounce the word 'German' is notorious).

- 'Nice day today, isn't it?' does not exist in German as a greeting. (Nor does it, for that matter, in the USA, where on one occasion I was almost physically attacked for uttering this sentence to a New York lift attendant who believed I was trying to wind him up). We refugees have learnt to understand the meaning of this phrase, but not necessarily that of its follow-up, 'Spring in the air!', to which one refugee is said to have replied, 'Vy should I?' ('Spring' in German is 'jump'.)

- A German Jewish couple at a grocery shop: 'We'd like some fruit drink.'
'Juice?'
Husband to wife: 'There you are, they are already starting here, too'.

- Friend to grandmother: 'Congratulations! I hear your grandson has been accepted for Oxford. What is he reading?'
'Oh, all sorts, *Gone with the wind, Suzy Wong ...*'

- And so as not to forget the classical scene: someone was asked whether he knew the English for the first line of Hamlet's soliloquy, and proudly quoted it: 'His or not his, that is the question' (A re-translation from the excellent transposition into German, 'Sein oder nicht sein'; 'sein' has a double meaning, 'to be' or 'his')

We developed after a time a mixture of languages of our own, which in imitation of 'Franglais' I might call 'Engman' or, if you prefer, 'Gerglish'. Many of us amused ourselves with literal translations of British words and sayings or expressions such as 'I must schon say', (a plaintive mixture of German and English), 'guest giver' for 'Gastgeber' (host), 'Schweizer Häuschen' for the London Swiss Cottage, around which the bulk of refugees lived; 'one sausages oneself halt through' (again a mixture of the two languages, 'sausage through ' being a verb for the German 'durchwursteln' = 'muddle through'.) 'This tie does not stand you' (the German verb 'stehen' can mean 'stand' or 'suit'). 'I cannot more, I break together' (a literal translation of the German 'I am at the end of my tether, I am having a breakdown'). Or, defensively about a woman who has become the object of malicious gossip: 'She is better than her cry.' (The German 'Ruf' may mean 'cry' or 'reputation'.) 'Gentlemen upon the ladies!' is the literal translation of an entirely proper German toast in honour of the female guests.

Some probably involuntary boobs were the way in which an employer dismissed an employee who would not mend his ways: 'I have told you once, I have told you twice – now it is so weit' ('now the time has come.') Or the waiter in a restaurant drawing a customer's attention to the fact that her scarf had fallen down: 'You dropped what.'

We also used literal translations of English expressions which could have a very strange sound in German – for instance 'Flaschenhals' for bottleneck. As someone said, bemoaning his somewhat haphazard use of the language: 'With mein English it is not so white hare' (a homonym of the German 'nicht so weit her', meaning not much to write home about.)

There was, of course, a non-linguistic kind of refugee humour too, though it was far less frequent. One of the nicest stories I remember is that of a refugee doctor who had just started his practice and was waiting for prospective patients to notice his existence. He wrote to a friend: 'Yesterday I had one patient. Today my consulting hours were a little quieter.'

Two friends meet. 'Have you got a job yet?' 'No, but I have hopes. Meanwhile I am polishing up my English'.

'Wouldn't it be better if you were to english up your Polish?'

The same friends are sitting on a bench in a park when a lark drops something on the head of one of them. Victim: 'And for the English he sings!'

III

Names presented problems in several ways. There were first of all those which in English are virtually 'impossible', such as 'Liachowsky', more than difficult to pronounce in English, let alone to remember; or those with a double meaning, such as 'Worms' (after an ancient and beautiful German town in which, inter alia, Martin Luther in 1521 defended his theses). Interestingly enough, though, I knew two refugees named Worms, both doctors who were sufficiently proud of their original name to keep it without alteration. I myself was, albeit not to the same degree, in a similar situation. English people would invariably spell my name 'Flesh', for which the German word is Fleisch, and English Jews would occasionally call me thus, apparently convinced that I had anglicised my name (which in fact derives from the German word 'Flasche', 'bottle'). 'Fleisch' does not always sound very attractive to German ears and therefore German refugees like to avoid saying it or even the English 'flesh'. Thus, a refugee lady, talking about her son, suddenly remembered that there was a member of the Flesch family among those present. In order not to sound offensive, she hastily referred to her offspring as 'my meat and blood'. Anyway, I kept my name and was pleased when my British-born children did the same.

But a great many people did anglicise their names or changed them altogether. I remember someone called Ellbogen (German for 'elbow') who did not translate it literally as he might have done, but quite cleverly changed its spelling so as to make it sound the same as before: Elboughan. In the same vein Hahn became Hawn and someone called Liebl (pronounced 'Leebl' in German) changed his name to Leigh-Bell. Rosenberg became Montrose, Schoenberg Beaumont. Another famous example was that of two brothers named Schwarzschild (Blackshield): One changed his name to Black, the other to Shield. Name changing became near-obligatory for all refugees who joined the army during the war, in particular the Pioneer Corps, without at that time having acquired British nationality. The idea was to give them some sort of protection in case they became prisoners of war and were executed by the Germans as spies. I have my doubts how much this would really have helped them, but fortunately, to my knowledge, the matter was not put to the test.

Some members of the army, as well as civilians, adopted, rather unjustifiably, very famous names such as Churchill, Nelson etc. For members of the Forces, the changes had to be approved by the commanding officer, and many got away with their near-blasphemous renaming. One man who was not so lucky was a soldier who wanted to call himself Clark Gable. He had some justification as his German name was Konrad Giebel (German for gable). Interesting that the name of a famous film star was more sacrosanct to that commanding officer than that of Nelson, a historical world figure! Adopting very English names did not always end well. Someone calling himself John Gay, for instance, may have come to regret it. Others had a certain amount of logic on their side. Someone over 6 ft tall called himself Longfellow. Braunberg became Browning, Schiller became Shelley etc. Someone with a good sense of the original called himself Anders (which in German simply means 'different'). Another, equally witty, called himself Werth. His original German name had been Wertheimer and, as he said, by dropping the 'eimer', he had 'kicked the bucket' (bucket = Eimer in German).

There was a story making the rounds about a refugee who changed his name to Shelter. The joke was that his previous name had been Liftschitz (which sounds Yiddish for the German word 'Luftschutz' = Air Raid Precautions). I believe there were no people who got their names by accident, but during previous immigrations this was apparently more likely to happen. The story goes of one immigrant who, when asked for his name, replied in his mother tongue with 'schon vergessen' ('already forgotten'), and ended up as 'Sean Ferguson'.

When you met a refugee with a very English and therefore obviously adopted name, you often played a mental game, trying to guess what he had been called originally. When eventually, rather tactlessly, you asked him whether your guess had been right, this could be embarrassing in cases where the person in question happened to be a British-born 'passport Englishman' and was resentful at having been mistaken for being non-British. Awkward situations in a different way could arise when the adopted name was a fairly common one and British-born people of the same name, on happening to hear it, asked its bearer which part of the family he belonged to. A friend of mine who had adopted the name 'Hilton' used to reply in those cases, 'The Irish Hiltons.' He always got away with it. Some people were too proud or found it unnecessary to make a change. One of them was a friend of mine named Fuchs. When he became naturalised, he announced, 'Now that I am an Englishman, I want my name to be pronounced the English way – Fucks.' Someone had to tell him the facts of life.

The name game was not only played by individuals. There were also commercial firms with names they would probably have avoided had they been longer in this country. The name of one of my clients invariably caused some amusement in the firm of Lloyd's brokers with whom I was co-operating at the time, proving that no profession is free from people looking for the double entendre where none is intended. The company was called 'Ram Accessories'. But the best one, to my mind, was the name with which a firm manufacturing precision engineering parts chose to describe its activities: 'True Screws'.

Not that native Britishers did not make fun of us in turn. I remember during the war, a bus conductor on a route through Hampstead, the district where most refugees congregated, calling out 'Finchley Road' as 'Curfewstendam' (Kurfürstendamm had been pre-war Berlin's Oxford Street, and the play on the word 'curfew', to which we refugees were subject, was obviously irresistible). Along similar lines is the story of a woman who is sitting on a bus when the conductor, collecting fares, steps heavily on her toes. Startled, she exclaims 'Verbrenn!' ('May you burn', one of the many colourful Jewish curses uttered by people against those they are annoyed with but wish absolutely no harm to). The conductor replies: 'Change at Golders Green' (which is near the best-known London crematorium).

Then there was the young Irish waitress employed in one of the restaurants mainly frequented by refugees, who claimed that she was quite unable to learn any foreign language. In spite of this handicap she had managed, through constant repetition, to retain two German phrases which German visitors to the restaurant, mostly Berliners, invariably greeted each other with: 'Tach, wie gehts?' 'Danke, Beschissen' ('How do you do?' 'Thanks, shitty'). Part of the joke lay in 'Tach', the very Berlinish abbreviation for 'Guten Tag' (good day).

Then there was the story of the bus load of refugees from Germany all being allocated to the same village until they could be dispersed. The reception committee was ready and did its best to make the arrivals welcome. One old man seemed particularly tired, staggering exhausted from his vehicle.

'You poor man, here, have a cup of tea. You must have had a terrible journey.'

'Yes, I'm afraid I did.'

'Where do you come from?'

'Dover. I'm the driver.'

Yes, times were difficult for us, but not without their light relief.

Customs, morals and similar matters

As I have already shown, whilst the unshakeable conviction of British superiority could not fail to rub off on us, there were sufficient matters that we wondered at and which at times even gave rise to harmless amusement.

Not the least of our puzzlement concerned sex and moral attitudes. Most people are convinced that their own country produces the best lovers, if not always the most alluring women, and has the most progressive or at least the most valid moral code. We grudgingly acknowledged that, if their reputation was anything to go by, Frenchmen and Italians might be considered superior. But that we were ahead of the British was certainly the firm belief held by many refugees from Germany when measuring themselves against them — I think with some justification. I should add that during the inter-war period the German middle classes had been by no means sexually promiscuous or less than scrupulously moral. In fact, the law did not allow anything else: during my German law studies in the 1920s we still learned that a mother had been sent to prison for the crime of procuring. What she had done was to have allowed her daughter's boyfriend, who had missed the last tram, to stay overnight. Equally, German censorship of books, plays etc was quite severe. Yet in spite of this I think it is true to say that in this area the British were far more backward. Some parts of British society had, during the mid-1930s, still not freed themselves from many Victorian attitudes and beliefs that were incredibly straight-laced and dated.

This view was certainly not held only in refugee circles. I have already mentioned GJ Renier's book, *The English, Are They Human?* Whether or not one agrees in every respect with what the author writes, the book represents the opinion of a clearly intelligent and observant foreigner resident in this country for many years and with a great affection for it. It is worth repeating that, since he was not a refugee, but lived here of his own volition, he was not disadvantaged by the same pressures we were under. Thus his opinions deserve to be taken seriously.

To quote just a few passages from his book (pp.76ff):

'Sex in England is considered a sinful thing and is taboo.'

'I once received a visit from a middle-aged solicitor who, at the end of the conversation, carefully edged his way behind my secretary's back for the express purpose of pointing at my French yellow-backs with a wink and a leer. To this very typical Englishman my innocent collection of 17th and 18th century French classics represented a naughty, alluring and forbidden world, the kind of thing one does not mention to "the wife". '

'It has taken me years of investigation to become convinced of the generally accepted fact that among people of the lower middle-class, coitus normally takes place only once a week and a special night of the week is set aside for this rite.'

Are these views exaggerated? Not, I believe, at that time. Of course, conditions today cannot be compared in any way with all that; but much of what Renier describes was indeed what we encountered when we arrived, and this was the foundation on which we formed our opinions about the subject of sex and mores in England generally.

I remember a particularly striking example about the latter when a friend and I were taking two young girls to lunch during the midday break at the Pitman Secretarial College in London, where they were both students. We boys were in our twenties and the two girls were about 18. We had already known each other for some time prior to emigration. On this occasion, we had entertained them at a cheap cafe – the cost of a meal in a halfway good restaurant would have been entirely beyond our means – and at the end of the allotted hour accompanied them back to their school, where we stood chatting at the entrance for a minute or two, a perfectly respectably-behaved and decently dressed little group.

There must have been at least 60 girls returning from lunch and milling around at the gate, but an eagle-eyed teacher watching the busy street saw us, fixed a malevolent stare on our companions and sharply called out to them, 'Come over here immediately!' They complied and were hauled without delay before the headmistress, who accused them of having damaged the school's reputation by being seen in the street talking to two young males. When they maintained that they had known us for quite some time and, in reply to a specific question by the headmistress, said they had been introduced to us by their parents, they were let off with a warning. 'If you were British, you would almost certainly have been expelled, but I am taking into account the fact that you are foreigners and have obviously not been brought up in the way befitting decent girls. But if it ever happens again ...'

Pitman's was one of the foremost secretarial colleges in the country and I know the story sounds unbelievable, but it is not the only one of its kind. I know of another Jewish immigrant, a young student nurse who had a somewhat similar experience. During night duty on her ward, she heard an old man who was very ill and only half-conscious murmur repeatedly, 'Bugger, bugger, bugger ...' Her linguistic knowledge did not extend to that expression, so next morning she asked the day sister to enlighten her. She was immediately instructed to report to the matron 'for insolence'. Only the fact that she could demonstrate that as a foreigner she had no idea what the word meant saved her from a severe reprimand, if not dismissal. All this is about on a par with the Victorian custom of draping the legs of grand pianos to avoid arousing sexual thoughts in the male members of the family. Piano legs of all things, I ask you; how repressed can you be! Seeing the changes in behaviour of young people today, the headmistress and ward sister in question must be in perpetual motion, revolving in their graves.

On another occasion I was looking for a part-time secretary. At that time half-day working on Saturdays was still the rule, but I was working at the offices of the Jewish National Fund which of course were always closed on the Sabbath. Being very busy, I needed to do some work outside office hours. I therefore telephoned a well-known employment agency and asked to be sent one or two secretarial applicants for an interview. 'Certainly. What is your office address?' Here I made my fatal mistake: 'As a matter of fact, the employment would be at my private residence, which is ...' I got no further: 'How dare you suggest such a thing! We are a respectable firm.' And the man at the other end of the line slammed down the receiver. I did not dare approach another agency in case I repeated the experience.

The point of the story is not so much the fact that apparently employment agencies did not send office personnel to private houses on principle (but then, what about domestics?) but the disproportionately violent reply to my request. These are not the reactions of people not interested in sex. On the contrary: they indicate an enormous sexual repression, linking even the most harmless manifestations of everyday life to this forbidden activity, even in thought.

It is not surprising that reports about such episodes made the rounds in our circles and caused us to draw our own conclusions about British sexual attitudes generally. I am afraid we judged the standard of English sex education mainly from the well-known advice given by a mother to her daughter when asked about the facts of life: 'Lie back and think of England.' To my knowledge, there is no equivalent saying in any other language. As a specific example of the lack of sex education, I remember my wife and I taking the 13-year-old daughter of English friends of ours by plane to a Continental holiday resort where she was to be reunited with her parents. When it came to the completion of the obligatory landing card she turned to my wife and asked: 'How should I answer "sex" - "child"?'

There is the equally famous saying, 'It's safe standing up.' This is of course not confined to Britain, but we held the opinion that only English girls still believed in it. And I remember my reaction when reading somewhere of a mother exclaiming: 'I'd rather see my daughter dead at my feet than her having an illicit affair!' I always wondered what I would have replied if the remark had been made in my presence. Hopefully I would have queried:

'Have you asked your daughter what she would prefer?'

Numerous, probably largely invented stories about the British sex life gained currency with us. A questionnaire for something or other asking: (a) 'Do you have sex regularly?' (b) 'If so, how often?' was answered by somebody with (a) 'Yes' and (b) 'Once a month.' This seems to confirm GJ Renier's opinion quoted earlier in this chapter. Or there is the somewhat tired story about remarks made by girls of various nationalities after sex. The German – as I have pointed out, by no means all that liberated at that period – gives a rueful 'Was werden Sie jetzt von mir denken!' ('What will you think of me now!'), the French girl a disappointed: 'C'est tout?' and the English girl a concerned 'Do you feel better now?' The girl in the joke obviously did not realise what sex was all about, and apparently considered it a therapeutic exercise.

As one more example, here is, with due apologies to my more refined readers, the somewhat coarse but certainly forthright reply of an English girl on being asked by a refugee to have sex with him. He told me the story himself: 'What for? It only makes you tired and me wet'. There was also the old joke – it resurfaced recently, claiming to be new – about a guest visiting a house occupied by two old spinsters and noticing a condom lying on the piano. Seeing his puzzled look, one of the ladies explains: 'We found this thing last year one morning in our garden. On the package it said, "Place on the organ to avoid infection." We don't own an organ so we put it on the piano. And do you know, we neither of us have had a cold since.'

Frowning upon unmarried sex was at that time not peculiar to Britain, of course. But it seemed there were degrees. We once employed an English char woman, a nice and decent girl, by no means without intelligence. She had a boyfriend whom she knew was married though living apart from his wife. One day she gave us notice. The reason: she was going to marry that man. 'But he's already married!' we protested, shocked.

'That doesn't matter.'

'Doesn't it? It is a crime and since you know about it, that probably makes you an accessory. So he can leave you at any time without risking your taking any steps against him. You may have children by him and you and they will be quite unprotected.'

But whatever we said made no impression. She considered a ring on her finger, however illegitimate, preferable to unmarried sex. So she went through a ceremony of marriage which she realised was null and void as well as illegal. I doubt that matters are taken to the same extreme in most other countries..

Not that British men didn't discuss sex or know their share of smutty jokes, but 'not in front of the ladies'. I suspect this was one of the reasons for the – in our eyes – quaint custom, at dinner parties, of the female guests retiring, leaving the men to themselves for some time so that the latter could let their hair down

To my knowledge, during their first few years in England, not many refugees had British girl- or boyfriends. One of the exceptions appears to have been an acquaintance of mine who had a notoriously successful sex life. However, having been warned about the risk of possible breach-of-promise actions, he always insisted on the girl in question confirming beforehand, in writing if you please, that he had not proposed marriage to her. I shall never know what he had got that I hadn't, which let him get away with it, but I take my hat off to him.

A further source of puzzlement for refugees, purely theoretically (they would not have been able to afford it) was the English attitude towards prostitution. British law did (and does) not take official account of the fact that the profession is as old as it is ineradicable and no doubt necessary. It was of course an offence for a prostitute to solicit, let alone 'do it' in a public place, though walking through Hyde Park at night during the summer – which at that time was still possible without the danger of being mugged; nobody entertained any such fears – it was evident that this particular prohibition did not seem to trouble a number of people unduly. So a prostitute had to take a room in which to conduct her business. The landlord from whom she was renting it could be found guilty of living off immoral earnings or running a brothel. If a prostitute solicited in a public place, she was liable to be arrested. On the other hand, if she accepted money and then reneged on the agreement, she was also committing a criminal act. Being a Peeping Tom was likewise an offence. Only the 'client' did not break the law at the time. As we know, today this is no longer quite correct either. For reasons whose logic, frankly, escapes me, a man must not under any circumstances try to find a prostitute whilst sitting in a car. It is OK as long as he finds one on foot. At any rate, the British attitude in this matter was and still appears to be typically ambivalent and not very thoroughly considered. Everybody agrees that, prostitution being inevitable, the best way of controlling it (ie reducing the number of pimps, sexually transmitted diseases and its nuisance factor in respectable neighbourhoods) would be to legalise brothels. But I doubt that parliament or local councils will ever be able to bring themselves to do anything so politically incorrect, however logical and realistic.

Yet this would have nothing to do with sexual morality as such, the view on which can be a lot stricter in other countries than in ours. This was, to my mind, never better illustrated than by the experience of a friend of mine, an MP, who on one occasion had to look after a Middle-Eastern trade delegation which for some reason was visiting Bath. On the first afternoon of their stay, he noticed members talking to one another in a rather agitated manner. Eventually the leader of the delegation turned to him and said: 'Could you please give us the address of a good brothel?' In Bath, of all places! The mind boggles, but should it? In any case, I can only hope that my friend's inevitably unhelpful reply did not have a too damaging effect on British export trade.

One of the arguments put forward against accepting female refugees into a country is the perceived danger of adding to prostitution, and this may well be right. It is worth mentioning that cases of German female refugees turning to prostitution were extremely rare – at least to my knowledge. I don't mean to moralise but, since making their living in this way is often the 'last resort' of women in dire straits, it does say something very significant about the resilience of female refugees from Nazi oppression that they preferred jobs as domestics, frequently working under almost impossible hardship and for next to no money.

In the British Army (in which, contrary to some other countries, there were and to my knowledge are no brothels), the sexual urges of soldiers and officers were apparently appeased by bromides introduced into army food. I have been told by members of the Forces that during the last war, they avoided army food prior to going on leave for that very reason.

Office life, too, was strictly regulated. In the large firm of Lloyd's Brokers in which I spent my first six months as a trainee, shorthand typists were strictly segregated from male employees; the latter were not allowed into the typing pool and in fact even occasional chats on the office premises between members of different sexes were not encouraged. The girls' frocks had to reach well below the knees and every dictator's desk had to have a 'modesty panel' so that the stenographer – there were, of course, no dictaphones yet, let alone word processors – sitting opposite him to take dictation did not have her legs exposed to view. What struck me as odd was the fact that in that firm every private office door had a peephole. People wanting to speak to the occupant would normally look through the hole before knocking, so as not to cause him unnecessary disturbance. At least this was the official reason. I have always wondered whether it was the only or real one; to me it seemed to be a severe intrusion into privacy. But at that time it was generally accepted and I never heard anyone object.

Enough of sex. There were plenty of other customs that appeared strange to us. One that we found most peculiar was the British attitude towards teeth. At that time it was considered the done thing to have them all pulled as early as possible so as to avoid future trouble. It is reminiscent of the medical practice, rampant early in the 20th century, of removing children's tonsils at an early age, something that has since been proved to be not only unnecessary but a potential health hazard. But it surely cannot be compared with removing all a person's teeth! Apart from everything else, the avoidance of future trouble was certainly a miscalculation: false teeth can cause severe gum trouble and after some time will need replacement either through wear and tear or owing to a change in the shape of the patient's mouth.

Yet I encountered several young colleagues who told me how much they were *looking forward* to reaching the age of 25 or so when they would have all their teeth out. There was absolutely no point in arguing with them; 'having one's teeth out' was simply axiomatic and not, as far as I know, confined to any particular class. I remember reading an advertisement picturing a very attractive, clearly upper-class (at that time it was still easily distinguishable) young lady on the telephone. It appeared that she had had the operation the day before; her friend at the other end of the line was congratulating her (!) and recommending some particularly soothing gargle – I was so struck, after all these years I even remember the name of the manufacturers: Milton – as a remedy against the inevitable soreness during the first few days.

Doctors seemed to be of the opinion that having one's teeth extracted was good for general health or at least a certain cure for various illnesses, and sometimes recommended it when they could not think of anything else. It was something like the advice which the medical profession used to give at the beginning of the 20th century to people suffering from depression: 'A few weeks in the country will do you the world of good.' Not infrequently it had the opposite effect; the country can be very depressing for townies.

We, being used to Continental dentists who put up a fierce fight for the preservation of every tooth, would (and not only for this reason) not have been seen dead in a British dentist's surgery. Opinions on the degree of favourable influence German/Jewish immigrants exerted on British culture, science, business and professional life vary widely and may well have been over-enthusiastic in some instances. But I believe there can be very little doubt that the influx of German dentists as a by-product of the refugee situation did have a profound effect on British dentistry. Not that refugee dentists always felt able to practise what they preached. My own dental surgeon, who had his consulting rooms in a posh London district, used to tell the story of a removal man, who happened to be working in the house next door, coming to him during the lunch break, obviously in some pain, pointing to one of his teeth and demanding its immediate removal. This was, of course, against all this dentist's professional principles, but the prospective patient was the size of a small tank and my friend felt that any protest would not only have been futile but possibly downright dangerous. So, without further ado, he gave the man a local anaesthetic and performed the operation. When it was over, the man got up, plonked 2/6d (12½ p) on the table and walked out. Clearly this was the customary tariff and may be a partial explanation for the frequency with which British dentists had to pull out teeth in order to scratch a living.

We had to get used to much else of a more minor nature. Take eating habits: cutting potatoes with a knife – taboo in Germany – certainly made life easier. On the other hand, the British way of eating soup and peas may have been more aesthetic but was certainly less practical than the Continental method of putting the soup spoon into one's mouth or heaping peas onto the fork. The pride of English hosts as they showed off their carving skills at the dinner table and let everybody's food get cold was for us always a source of some irritation. Having the main meal in the evening instead of at lunchtime was another difference we needed to adjust to. Eating it at midday is presumably healthier, but this was linked to the fact that in Germany there was no need to hurry one's luncheon as most shops and offices closed for one to two hours during that time, an often irritating custom. Of course, it would have been impossible in London for office workers to go home for lunch.

One custom we found very sensible was the British weekend dress code once we had got used to it. Initially, on the rare occasions when we were invited by 'genuine Englishmen' and turned up in our Sunday best, we were usually amazed to be confronted by our hosts attired in their oldest clothing. Comfort was the obvious watchword, and rightly so. The same applied to taxi drivers who, judging by their clothing, seemed to be on a perpetual weekend. In Berlin at that time, most wore smart chauffeur uniforms.

Another surprise was the fact that smoking in cinemas and theatres was generally permitted. This had certainly not been the case at home – not, of course, on account of any anti-smoking sentiments, which at the time did not exist, but simply as a means of fire prevention. The lighting-up of hundreds of cigarettes in a cinema as soon as someone started smoking on the screen was an entirely new phenomenon for us, initially one we disapproved of but, after some hesitation, adopted as a matter of course. I recall puffing away at a theatre performance when an elderly man sitting next to me asked me to stop. As I remember, I was rather surprised and somewhat put out about this imposition. However, when he explained that he had been gassed during the war and was asthmatic, I magnanimously complied. In such a case one had to make allowances, however unreasonable the request! In this particular matter the world has certainly gone from one extreme to the other. But, while the rules about smoking were more than lax, the obligatory lowering of the safety curtain in theatres during the interval seemed to us to be overcautious. There was even insurance against the curtain not coming down due to a technical fault, which would have meant abandoning the second part of the performance. Continental and British fire precautions clearly differed. But, as far as I know, the incidence of accidental fires in theatres and cinemas was no more or less frequent in England than it had been in Germany.

Drinking laws were another source of puzzlement to us, not only on account of the licensing laws (unintelligible to any foreigner), but also because pubs in Germany were 'Kneipen', establishments comparable to transport caffs here. A surprising fact was also that newsagents were allowed to sell cigarettes and tobacco. And in Germany, a chemist was a chemist was a chemist. Selling cosmetics was not really regarded as professional. This was the job of the *Drogerie*. But, of course, there weren't any in this country.

The concentration of trades and professions – doctors, lawyers, jewellery wholesalers etc crowded into certain districts – was equally new to us. The fact that a prominent lawyer or medical specialist worked from home did not – in Berlin, for instance – give any adverse indication of his status. Nor did the choice of district in which you lived indicate your social standing anything like as clearly in Germany as it did here.

These examples will show the innumerable strange

differences to which we often had problems adjusting. But whatever else can be said about them, they kept us on our toes.

War

I

On September 3rd, 1939, practically all refugees from Naziism became enemy aliens. Again, I have to preface this chapter with a personal remark, as my case was not quite typical. Of course, like every German Jew, I had lost my German nationality. However, since at my birth my father had been a Hungarian citizen, I had automatically acquired his nationality. As a non-German I could not have completed my law studies, hence in 1930 our whole family had become naturalised Germans. The date is not without significance. It shows that even at that time nobody took the possibility of Hitler ever achieving power into serious consideration. Had we done so, we would, of course not have taken on German nationality. When the Nazis did become the governing party, I enquired with the Hungarian Embassy in Berlin what steps I would have to take in order to reacquire my original nationality. To my agreeable surprise I was told that, according to Hungarian law, I had not lost my citizenship and thus had dual nationality.

Whilst still living in Germany, it would, of course, have been the sensible step to ask for a Hungarian passport right away and to carry it with me at all times. For, during that initial Nazi period, non-German Jews were still largely left unmolested. However, since I was also a German – the general deprivation of citizenship was yet to be decreed – the idea of having two passports did not appeal to me and I arranged instead for the Hungarian one to be sent to the embassy in Holland, where I intended to emigrate shortly. Again, the opinion we had formed about the threat of the Nazi regime and its stability is significant: I did not consider it necessary to take the obvious precaution of carrying a foreign passport. We still had no full understanding of the precariousness of the situation we had been landed in and tended to grossly underestimate it.

I lost my German nationality only some time after I had moved from Holland to England. Thus at the outbreak of war I was not an enemy, but a neutral alien. In this way the internment of former Germans and Austrians decreed in 1940 passed me by. When, after a few years, Hungary entered the war on the side of the Germans, this emergency measure had long become a thing of the past unless, of course, there existed any special reason for it. Here again I had been lucky: during the first few weeks of the war, I had received a circular from some Hungarian political organisation asking me to sign a declaration expressing my support of, and loyalty to, the British cause. Since the document was in Hungarian, of which I did not speak a word (except 'I love you'), I had written back to say that I would be only too glad to sign the paper once I knew what exactly it was I was supposed to lend my signature to. Would they therefore kindly let me have a translation? I never received a reply. When Hungary became an enemy country, it turned out that the organisation in question was suspected of harbouring a number of fifth columnists. Many signatories to the original declaration were therefore investigated and a few interned. So mine was one of the rare cases when not knowing a foreign language turned out to be an advantage.

I had no inclination to 'join' the Hungarian community in order to enjoy any possible privileges of neutrality, but felt and acted entirely as what I was: an ex-German refugee. With hindsight, it seems strange and even foolish to me not to have taken advantage of the happy coincidence of my neutral status. But at the time it simply did not occur either to my wife or myself. Solidarity among refugees was, quite subconsciously, a matter of course. And anyway, apart from the internment question, the accident of my birth would have made very little practical difference – though, I should add, one could not know this at that time. But when, in the first flush of excitement, somewhat to my own surprise, I volunteered for service in the British army and, of course, had to mention the fact that I had formerly been a German national, my application, like those of all other German refugees at that time, was turned down. When the practice changed, I had already joined the official war work training scheme and was employed by a factory producing war material. I can assert with every confidence that my failure to become a soldier was no loss whatever to the British army.

Obviously, at the time when the outbreak of war was in the balance, we refugees had been in an ambivalent position. On the one hand we were hoping as fervently as everybody else that peace would be preserved; in fact, probably even more strongly, because we had witnessed at first-hand some of the thorough and unceasing efforts on the part of the German regime to rebuild its military strength and war potential. This was happening under the very noses of the Allies who did nothing to counteract the breaches of every restriction they had originally imposed on Germany after the First World War. We could therefore appreciate rather better than the ordinary non-German man in the street the wide gap in the material and psychological preparedness of the two potential contestants. On the other hand, none of us was in favour of appeasement which was still being practised by the Allied Governments and supported by many leading politicians. We belonged to the minority who knew by now that any concession would be futile. We eagerly read the frequent articles (in the *Evening Standard,* I believe) by Winston Churchill, who at that time was still in the wilderness, recognised the danger better than most and could give expression to his insights in his inimitable forceful style. There was, of course, nothing we ourselves could actively do in this matter even if we had been so minded. Our position was sufficiently precarious as it was and our best policy was to keep as low a profile as possible.

An additional and very real worry for many of us was the fate of any relatives still in Germany and, for all of us, our personal position in the event of war. About the first, we could do little. It had become more and more difficult to get Jews out of Germany and into this country. As for ourselves, we anxiously speculated whether the fact that we no longer possessed German nationality would make any difference to the authorities here. Would there be a distinction between ourselves and the gentile Germans who were living in this country, not a few of them probably Nazis or Nazi sympathisers? We were pessimistic. The authorities would still regard us as enemy aliens, and not without reason: it was almost unimaginable that some fake refugees would not have been planted among us by the German secret service.*

* How strongly this opinion was held in some circles can be shown by a speech made by Mavis Tate MP in the House of Commons in July 1940, as quoted in the book *A Bespattered Page?* by Ronald Stent, published by

Interestingly enough, as far as I am aware, no case came to general knowledge, except one false alarm: the arrest, during the first days of the war, of a very prominent refugee who had for some time after his emigration been able to remain the local representative of a large German industrial concern. Refugees who knew him were convinced from the outset that it was all a ghastly mistake. I too knew this man and fully shared that opinion. On the other hand, isn't the mark of a successful spy that nobody should have any idea of his or her dual role? Looked at in this way, nobody, however unlikely, could really be beyond suspicion. At any rate, to everybody's relief, the British authorities realised within a few days that it had all been a mistake and the suspect was set free without a stain on his character.

But what about the British population at large? A German accent might well be sufficient to evoke hostility or even active physical aggression. Stories about the First World War were revived in which, so we heard, even German dachshunds had been attacked in the streets as their owners took them out to do their business. But even if people appreciated that we were as genuinely anti-German as any Englishman, might they not accuse us of having 'started the war' – as if we could have done! – or at least of having encouraged it purely as a Jewish revenge act against the German people? We felt convinced that this idea would be fostered by German propaganda for all it was worth as part of psychological warfare. And, of course, everybody realised that sooner or later there would almost certainly be bombing of civilians. How would the British react in that case?

André Deutsch, 1980: 'It is no good saying that because a person is a refugee or Jew, he may not nevertheless be a danger to this country.'

Disregarding internment – on which some comments later – I think I am right in saying that, when it came to it, very little of what we feared happened. The Germans did not seem to realise that we might be of considerable value to the British war effort and, surprisingly, did not try to sow suspicion against us. During the 'phoney war', when nothing much went on, there was in any case next to nothing that could have incensed the population against us. And more and more of us had already given living proof that we were wholeheartedly behind the war effort. And when the Blitz did start, there was just no question: everybody, without exception, was in the same boat. I can recall only two cases of open hostility against me: one as early as during the crisis in 1938 before Munich, when an old man tried to attack my wife and me in the street when he overheard us talking with German accents (nobody would have been so foolish as to speak German in public, and it was avoided even in private conversations). The other was in connection with my war work, to which I shall briefly refer later.

I personally never heard the accusation that, without us, the war would not have started. And indeed, the idea that the Jews and their unfortunate fate could have even remotely influenced the Allies when they were considering whether to declare war or not was just too ludicrous to be entertained by anybody except blind fanatics. The political reasons for the war were manifold and complicated, but the Jewish question played no part either in reality or in the minds of the British Government. And the British public readily followed the official line that after the German invasion of Poland it would just have been impossible to let Hitler get away a second time with what he had done to Czechoslovakia after

Munich.

Everybody had of course been fully aware of Hitler's hatred of the Jews, but as far as non-Jews were concerned, this knowledge was based only on newspaper and indirect eye-witness accounts. True, there had been, in peacetime, the occasional documentation in the shape of newsreels in cinemas – usually very vague in comparison to what is offered in today's TV news programmes. It is sometimes asserted that the reaction outside Germany would have been very different if at that time there had already been television coverage and everybody could have regularly seen the horrors that were being inflicted on German Jews.

Regretfully, I have to say that in my opinion this would almost certainly not have been the case. We have since had every opportunity of witnessing the unspeakable atrocities visited on the racial minorities of many countries, the unrelieved suffering caused by ethnic cleansing, the bodies discovered following indiscriminate killings of innocent civilians and whatever other bestial acts war criminals commit. Our governments condemn them, we ourselves, unless we are dedicated charity workers, salve our consciences by responding more or less generously to the various appeals for charitable contributions, but by and large that is all. The general public would simply not approve of any forcible official action going beyond mere words, at least unless it could be quite certain that this would not involve any danger to life and limb of British soldiers, let alone civilians; that there would be no risk of retaliation; and – I am sorry if this sounds offensive – profitable trade relations were not being affected to any marked extent. What better proof than Kosovo? Our military experts thought it would be much easier than it turned out to be to punish the Serbs without any real risks to ourselves, but even so there were a great many voices of dissent and by no means only for humanitarian reasons. And there has certainly never been any thought of taking similar action against Russia and China for the crimes they have committed against humanity.

I hate having to say it, but this scenario is as realistic as it is inevitable. For effective action would not only be impossible, but might even ignite a new world conflict. 'And for what?' the man in the street would ask. 'People we had never heard of till now and whose internal conflicts are not the business of outsiders, least of all us.' Not to mention the resulting enormous additional influx of refugees, which would be anything but welcome.

Nor, I am firmly convinced, would direct action have been of use to or even welcomed by the persecuted minorities themselves. Again, Kosovo has shown only too clearly what every German Jewish refugee could have told the various governments from the outset: aggression against the torturers is of no help whatsoever to the victims in their power. They are the ones supposed to be saved but the outside powers are quite unable to help them. In fact, quite the opposite: far from ameliorating their position, it is bound to destroy more of them than it can preserve. By the same token, if Germany had been attacked by the Allies on account of its anti-Semitism – an impossible proposition anyway – I am in no doubt that every, and I mean every, Jew in Germany would have been massacred forthwith.

It is often said that, during the last war, the Allies knew at quite an early stage what was really going on in Belsen, Auschwitz and all the other death camps. They are not infrequently blamed for not having taken any action to prevent it – unjustly so, I believe. Yes, they probably did know. But there was, first of all, the question of how this might have fitted in with the overall strategy of the war. If it had not, public opinion inevitably would have been strongly against it. This can be shown quite clearly by the attitude we all adopted when the V1 and V2 bombs were directed against London after the second front had been established. The army knew the locations of most of the launching pads but everybody, including us, the victims, was agreed that the Allied overall strategic plans should take precedence. We did not want them disrupted in any way to deal with the threat to us civilians. I know it is true that we, the potential victims, would have strongly disapproved of it.

But leaving this aside, what could the Allies have done? Bombed the camps? In spite of their sufferings, few if any of the Nazis' victims would have thanked them for it. It would not only have killed Jews and their tormentors indiscriminately but, again, it would have spelt the end of all the captives who had not by then perished under the Allied attacks or the routine gassings. Bombed the railway lines? What do you think would have happened to the Jews being transported in cattle trucks so overcrowded and insanitary that many died in transit? Would they have been taken care of? Of course not. It would only have prolonged and intensified their ordeal. The inescapable, terrible, unpalatable truth is that neither Jews nor any other persecuted minorities in whatever country can count on really effective outside help if their own governments are determined to destroy them.

II

Initially, the main practical consequence of the outbreak of war was the 'Tribunals' classifying enemy aliens according to the perceived danger they might represent, and the restrictions imposed on them and aliens generally. Those of us who were subject to curfew had to be indoors from, if memory serves me right, 9pm onwards. The strictness with which this was enforced varied somewhat. As my wife was expecting our first baby, we had moved to a small town about 40 minutes' drive from London (there was as yet no petrol rationing). The local police considered us to be harmless and tended to look the other way when we were seen in the streets a few minutes after the Cinderella hour due to the fact that the last but one performance at the local cinema finished only shortly after 9pm. On the other hand, when I applied on one occasion for permission to stay the night in London, as I wanted to work late at the office, this request was not only flatly refused but shortly before midnight of the day in question a policeman knocked on our door to check that I really was at home and had not transgressed the injunction.

Curfew was a minor inconvenience and readily accepted. Initially, we were all relieved that our worst fears about developments concerning us had not materialised. Hopefully the Germans might recognise that the Channel, the Maginot line and the Dutch dikes were making any penetration impossible and nothing untoward would be developing in the West. I know that today this sounds most unrealistic, but at that period of the war the most inexpert and ridiculous opinions were being printed and believed. One of them, which I have reason to remember, was a brief newspaper item about an interview with a Jewish refugee who, coming from Holland prior to the invasion of that country, had just landed in the USA, which at that time was still neutral. He had been a fighter pilot in the German Air Force during the 1914-18 war and predicted with absolute certainty, based on his intimate knowledge of German mentality and military conditions past and present, that Germany would collapse within the next three months. This was very heartening, until I read his name, which was mentioned in the news item: he happened to be related to me by marriage and had indeed been a fighter pilot during the first World War, had even received the *Pour le Merite* order, another recipient having been Hermann Goering. But his war experiences had left their mark. He was known in the family as a paranoiac of the first order, a most unreliable and unbalanced fantasist in every way and certainly without a shred of knowledge, expert or otherwise, about conditions in the German military establishment of the day. And the newspaper in question? It was the (then as now) highly regarded *Daily Telegraph*. The paper had considered the interview to be of sufficient importance to publish it in its 'stop press' section on the front page. So much for what you could believe at that time.

The East, of course, was a different matter, but although the invasion of Poland had been the event that had triggered off the declaration of war, it was remote and somewhat nebulous in the public mind. Also, here again, the most bizarre ideas about relative military strengths were current. I suspect, for instance, that any knowledge outside Finland about the Russian invasion of that country during the early months of the war is today confined mainly to questions in 'Trivial Pursuit'. And very few people outside Finland seem to remember the heroic resistance of that country against the invaders and its initial military successes mainly due, no doubt, to its geographic and weather conditions which lent themselves ideally to guerrilla warfare and surprise attacks. But, more interestingly, everybody seems to have repressed the memory of the fact that at the time the British public began to take seriously articles and letters in the press which discussed the possibility, even desirability, of sending a British expeditionary force to help the Finnish army complete its victory over the Russians who, let it be remembered, were during that period supportive of the Germans but not at war with us. Needless to say, after a few months all Finnish resistance was crushed by the overwhelming Russian might.

I will not insult the intelligence of the British authorities by suggesting that the idea of military intervention was ever even remotely entertained by the government or the High Command, but the fact that we, the people in the street, took any such nonsensical speculations at their face value shows the extraordinary lack of realism prevalent during the first phase of the conflict. This certainly also applied to my wife and myself. When our baby son was six months old, we decided that there was no good reason why we should not move back to London. Obviously nothing was going to happen. We were back in London on the very day the nightly bombing attacks started.

III

The Blitz has been the subject of innumerable learned and detailed descriptions, but to my knowledge less frequently from the refugees' point of view. One may ask whether there was, in this respect, any particular difference between the reaction and behaviour of refugees and those of British citizens. Not, I think, on the face of it. We were in it as completely as everybody else and tried to cope in the same way. We did what we could to help the war effort and all this was readily acknowledged by the population generally – and why not, seeing that we fully and unreservedly strove to identify with them. This had nothing to do with the purely formal question of whether we had at that time already become British naturalised citizens or not. Among a group of people in nightly danger of their lives, individual private backgrounds and circumstances cease to have any relevance. As I have already mentioned at the beginning of this chapter, I personally cannot recall a single hostile incident, caused by the Blitz on London, aimed either at myself or any of my friends. So, *were* there any differences in some directions? Well, yes, I can think of a few.

First of all, the internments. While our fellow citizens accepted us, there were instances where the authorities did not. The curfew, as far as it was still being enforced, was a comparatively minor irritation. The internment introduced after the collapse of France was definitely very much more than that. Naturally, no-one could deny that there was a case for it. Fifth columnists had obviously – though probably not as decisively as was alleged at the time – played their part in the downfall of France; not by causing it – the French had seemingly needed no outside help for that – but by adding to the general confusion and disruption. Invasion of England was a real possibility. It was only reasonable for the British to try to eliminate a potential danger that was perceived as having played an important part in the downfall of France. But of course, all of us knew that any suspicions against genuine refugees were completely groundless. To be treated as potential enemies was therefore apt to test our loyalty quite severely. That it did no permanent damage to it was, I believe, due to three reasons: firstly, we were sufficiently objective to see the point of the exercise; secondly, it was carried out in a mainly humane and civilised way — not forgetting various grave exceptions — and, once the immediate danger had receded, the authorities tacitly admitted their mistake and reversed their attitude to the full; and thirdly, the often very haphazard manner of its execution could sometimes even appeal to one's sense of humour.

Although I myself was spared any direct experience of this particular trauma, like everybody else I lived with the problems and anxieties of so many of my friends and was therefore, albeit indirectly, equally involved in them. The first thing to be said is that, understandably, it was a panic measure. The second, perhaps somewhat less understandably, is that decisions about who and who not to intern were often arrived at in an exceedingly amateurish manner. At the beginning of the war, Tribunals had been established to place enemy aliens into various categories, A, B and C. Among the persons who had the relevant decisions in their hands were people who could not really help the war effort in other ways — retired magistrates, blimpish old army personnel and others. Many of them had probably never before encountered a refugee, let alone possessed any clue of what they were really looking for; and often they had not been given sufficient general guidance either. Not a few of them therefore, appeared to be making up their own rules as they went along.

There was little doubt about A, the German non-refugees. The difference between B and C was mainly one of restrictions of movement, which frequently depended on rather irrelevant factors. I remember the case of a father (too old for work) and his son who had to travel around the county. The latter was given the most liberal grade, C. When it came to the father, the magistrate said, 'Well, you don't need to travel, so for you a B will be sufficient.' Slightly lopsided thinking, perhaps, but fair enough; no harm done, or so one thought. In other cases, people were made B because they had been residing in districts which had become areas of strategic importance and from which they were now understandably barred. Again, usually not the greatest piece of logic but not particularly important, one supposed.

Not so. The trouble was that, once internments began, the question of B and C was often decisive. In the above-mentioned case of father and son, for instance, the father was interned, the son was not. Other anomalies arose: a friend of mine was arrested by a policeman with whom he had, for many months, done service during the nights as an officially appointed air raid warden. On the other hand, it was not entirely unknown in less 'severe' cases for exceptions to be made on personal or compassionate grounds. Whilst this was very welcome, it might often have gone too far in the opposite direction. Any experienced spy or saboteur could have construed an appropriate case with ease.

Of course, on the face of it, the action was very successful – fifth columnists were certainly not a feature of the war in Britain – but I think it can be said without fear of contradiction that this was not due to the efficiency of the internment process, but to the fact that there simply weren't any saboteurs amongst the refugees. As I mentioned already, I believe it was this very amateurishness that took away much of the sting of the procedure. This and one additional factor: how the act of internment itself was handled by the police. In most cases, there was no midnight knock at the door and often no immediate arrest either. In some instances the police would even come and ask a refugee to be at the police station on a certain day at a certain hour to be interned. Also, the time when the policemen called was usually in the early morning. Many people made it their business to go for long walks at that time, in this way missing the police visit. Surprisingly, not all these cases were followed up so that some refugees avoided internment by this simple expedient. Thus, all in all, it was not handled very professionally.

Internment itself was in the majority of cases humane, too. In fact, in later years, it could sometimes be quite amusing to be present when former internees happened to meet and talk about their experiences. You might have thought you were at a school reunion of old boys of the class of '41. The exceptions were those who were quite unnecessarily, and as far as I know entirely haphazardly, sent to Australia or Canada. Not only did the German navy attack some of these transports, sometimes with tragic results, but the military personnel on board were of the lowest grade and often not only lacked any understanding, but were in fact deliberately brutal and also not above stealing from their charges. In my profession as an insurance broker, I dealt with a number of cases in which clients of mine had previously taken out annual travel insurance and were able to claim for the losses they sustained in this way. It has to be acknowledged that the insurers paid up in these cases without a quibble.

Inevitably, there was a good deal of hardship for many of the families who had suddenly lost their breadwinners. Wives and mothers (as long as they were not, which happened far less frequently, interned themselves) had to go out to work and/or where necessary were supported by Woburn House. Businesses founded by refugees who had in the first place built up a clientele consisting of fellow refugees had their own difficulties. If the majority of your clients are suddenly taken out of circulation, this is not exactly conducive to economic success, both as regards new business and payment of outstanding premiums. On top of it, those refugee firms which had employees who were interned – and that applied to most of us, because we obviously engaged refugees more readily than did British firms – normally did what they could to continue paying salaries to the families concerned. Luckily, matters returned to normal after a few months. Many internees volunteered for the army. The others were freed anyway and were glad to return to their families. Most of those sent abroad braved the dangers of the return journey; significantly, among them were many single men without family ties who nevertheless preferred being in the UK to the relative security of the countries overseas in which they would have been allowed to remain had they so wished. Some did and built up a new existence there.

In brief, internment was a very important albeit impermanent factor in keeping refugees apart from the rest of the population. But it was not the only one. Interestingly enough, there seems to have been a difference in the attitude of refugee families on the question of whether or not to evacuate their children from London during the Blitz. To my knowledge, comparatively few of them took advantage of this possibility. Understandably they found the idea of creating yet another situation in which children were separated from their parents too difficult to deal with. For this reason, some families even preferred to evacuate from London as a unit; in others the mother went with the children. But the majority, as far as I knew, kept their children with them during the time of greatest danger. I myself could never understand this attitude of 'If we are killed, it will be best for the children to go with us.' What selfish nonsense to think that for a child death is preferable to becoming an orphan!

Moreover, these parents never seemed to appreciate that death was by no means the only danger; there might be injuries, physical or psychological, that could maim a child for life. One of their arguments was that a separation could damage a child psychologically. True, but this was largely avoidable with proper explanations and regular contact. Moreover, it was curable. I strongly feel that these parents did not get their priorities right. For me, our innocent baby son being in London was a constant worry. The day my wife and I succeeded in evacuating him to helpful friends in the country belongs in the category of 'my happiest memories of the war'. And no psychological problems ensued.

Britishers and refugees alike were concerned about their relatives; but while the British worried about their menfolk overseas on active service, we were desperately anxious for our families left back home, necessarily passive at the hands of the Nazis.

Another difference was our general outlook. Jews

are pessimistic by nature as well as experience and for a long time events proved that, as far as the war was concerned, this outlook was abundantly justified. Some of us – I have to confess, myself included – even went so far as to try and obtain poison in case it came to the worst and the invasion we all thought imminent was successful. Thus we were frequently amazed to observe the optimism of the British in the face of obvious calamity. I have never been able to decide whether this was a character trait or simply caused by the fact that the bulk of the population did not recognise the true state of affairs. Probably a mixture of the two. The most striking example I can remember was the comment by an Englishman to whom my partner and I were giving a lift on the day France surrendered: 'Now at least we know where we stand.' Big deal!

But these differences apart, I think we did feel the same as everybody else. Basically, any situation of general stress, emergency or strong emotion affecting a homogenous group of people is apt to create a psychological state transcending that of the individual. This, of course, can work both ways. Panic will spread and affect everybody, an emotional experience of any kind likewise. This reaction can be triggered off by the most diverse situations – from a Nazi rally (for Germans!) to girls uncontrollably screaming in unison at a pop concert; from the death of a generally venerated person to a war situation. They all may cause a state of mind in a large number of individuals which would not occur if these same individuals were on their own – not necessarily physically but mentally.

During the war the trigger was the mortal danger threatening us all. I have never seen active service but

I believe that the acceptance of mass slaughter in the trenches during the First World War would not have been possible if the participants had not been motivated by something stronger than individual feelings and decisions. A member of the armed forces who opted out was liable to face a court martial and possible execution by firing squad. One might think, therefore, that sticking it out and going over the top was regarded as the lesser evil. But during the Blitz there was no such penalty for cowardice. It was possible to remove oneself from danger by evacuating from the most obvious target areas. Considering that not many individuals are outstandingly brave, it is surprising how comparatively few civilians did. They behaved in a manner which, though one should not call it 'heroic', certainly showed a disregard of danger which with hindsight we are inclined to find inexplicable, if not downright foolish.

And it was not even necessary to leave London. There was another option at night, the time of the greatest danger – the London underground shelters. The German bombs released over London during the early years were usually not of sufficient strength to penetrate into the London underground, so that anybody sheltering there was relatively safe, though there were several tragic exceptions. Of course, official figures were not available but it was reasonable to assume that the average number of people killed in London each night was not fewer than 50 – statistically a tiny proportion of the population, but undoubtedly a figure (1500 per month!) which should have made everybody consider very seriously whether it would not be preferable to accept the obvious inconveniences of the near-complete safety afforded. And a great many people did so, in the first place those who had been bombed out or lived in particularly affected London districts. The authorities certainly gave them all the help possible, bunks, soup kitchens, even a certain amount of entertainment, etc. But compared with the total population, they were a tiny minority. Most people did not think it worth their while to go to the 'trouble' of taking a potentially life-saving action – myself included. I regard myself as anything but brave; yet when I travelled home in the evening by underground and saw the hundreds of people in their bunks at every station, I almost felt a sense of superiority towards them. Utterly and completely unjustified as well as foolish, but there it was.

You cannot really understand it unless you have been in that situation yourself, and with hindsight not even once the situation has passed. I remember with genuine embarrassment an occasion when I was visiting a few clients in the West End. As it happened, I had an hour to spare before my next appointment and it was too early to go to a restaurant and have lunch. So I decided to spend the free time in one of the small news (and nothing else!) cinemas popular in London before the advent of TV. These places were usually underground. Sitting in the auditorium, I saw the obligatory message being flashed on the screen: 'An air raid warning has just sounded.' Being underground, I was almost completely safe. If a bomb had hit the building, we would have been buried under the rubble but quite likely have been dug out more or less unharmed. Yet, it was unthinkable that I should be discovered, whether dead or alive, to have been visiting a cinema during office hours, however legitimate the reason. So I left and went above ground. Facing possible bombs was preferable to the embarrassment of people thinking I had been wasting valuable working hours. And I remember the case of a lady leaving a communal air raid shelter while a raid was in progress, if you please, because there was a mouse running around.

Part of the explanation for such extraordinary behaviour may have been the feeling 'It can't happen to me'. For personal courage, I have to confess, did evaporate to a marked extent when one was exposed to acute danger. We all experienced this during attacks by VIs, the unmanned buzz bombs, during the latter part of the war. These missiles made a great deal of noise, but before falling they cut out. So you heard the noise, dived under the next available table and waited. There, the noise stopped! The next five seconds were the critical ones. Where had the bomb been, overhead or some distance away? The sound of an explosion far off – a sigh of relief. The danger had passed. I must confess no thought was given to the unfortunates who had been the victims that time.

All this may not quite tally with what I have written before about our desire not to disrupt the war strategy by attacking these sites before all else, but these contradictions did co-exist. And even amid danger, you did remain calmer than normal. I experienced this in the midst of one raid, returning one evening from having visited our son in the country. We travelled by bus through South London, notoriously far more heavily affected by the raids than North London, where we lived. There were fires all around us, streets closed, explosions nearby, yet our bus carried on regardless. And the air raid wardens on duty were so calm and matter-of-fact that I remarked to my wife, 'They must obviously be used to this sort of thing. It just shows how much more severely South London is affected than the North.' I was quite wrong. It subsequently turned out – though the papers of course did not report it in so many words – that this had been the first of the series of really severe fire raids on London, causing untold damage and many casualties.

Crime, though not absent, was greatly reduced. The heartfelt cry of a present-day grandmother is well known: 'I don't know what the world is coming to. You can't go out in the evenings any more for fear of being mugged. In my youth, during the war, the streets were completely safe.' Too true. The possibility of being attacked in the evenings simply did not occur to anyone. The main danger, so malicious tongues asserted, were the ambulances, often driven by young society girls who, judging by their own accounts, were rather accident prone, particularly during the blackout. (Curiously enough, I myself found blackout driving not at all stressful. I have never been a sailor but imagine that driving in the London blackout may have been similar to navigating a boat at sea during the night.)

Altogether, normal standards did not apply. I did war work for a time as a wages clerk. This involved my going round on Friday nights during the night shift, carrying an open tray with about 100 envelopes containing all the workers' weekly wages in cash. During that time, hardly a night passed without an air raid warning, which made it necessary for all lights to be extinguished. Usually this happened just at the beginning of my round. There I stood in the dark with loads of cash, the equivalent of two years' income for an individual, thus well worth banging me over the head for, surrounded by night shift workers, many of whom were 'at the rough end' of society. I never felt a moment's fear (except as I write this, in retrospect!). All in all, it was a most extraordinary time.

IV

So, what did refugees do during the war? There was no compulsion to join the army or do any war work. I don't know any statistics, but I doubt that the percentage of those refugees actively involved in the war effort as civilians was markedly different from that of British-born citizens. This may have been partly due to the fact that many of the latter were in, or deliberately went into, reserved occupations that exempted them from service in the armed forces, a consideration of no interest to refugees who were glad to get any work, whether in a reserved occupation or not. And for some of them war work may have been the first real job they were allowed to accept and thereby make a living.

A considerable number of refugees volunteered for the army. Originally they were allowed only into the Pioneer Corps who were not really a fighting force, though some of them did see front line service. The aim of most refugees was to be transferred to the regular army and quite a number succeeded. Some, owing to their knowledge of German, achieved comparatively high rank. (This qualification was not a feature that impressed the Pioneer Corps. There is the well-known story of the sergeant addressing a new intake of recruits: 'Which of you speak English fluently?' A few raised their hands, hoping for a job in line with their qualifications. 'OK, you go and clean the latrines, the others go off to English lessons.')

Others with special skills or knowledge did, once they had left the pioneer corps, intelligence or scientific work that was very useful to the war effort. Many others volunteered for work in war factories, which necessitated some initial training in Government Training Centres. I can testify from personal experience that the training was not very effective, at least for people like myself who are devoid of any technical aptitude whatever. There was a practical test at the end of the training period, which I passed only with the help of some colleagues who took pity on me. But it did not matter much whether you passed or not. Usually, we only got unskilled jobs anyway.

I ended up as a checker in the 'Goods In Department' of a factory, examining whether various parts manufactured by subcontractors were up to standard. I took this work very seriously. The quality of the stuff coming from these subcontractors, many of whom were one-man firms with very little technical skills themselves, was often quite appalling. I therefore disqualified a great many of the parts that came in. This almost cost me my job. The foreman of my section, seeing what I was doing, accused me of trying to sabotage the war effort! The goods in question were electrical precision hand tools, such as drills, screwdrivers etc, intended to enable tank crews to make running repairs. There must have been not a few cases of products approved by the foreman which proved to be useless. But at that time people could get away with substandard work quite easily. My experience of the unreasonable suspicion with which some circles regarded refugees was the exception but not an isolated one. I know of a young refugee girl, a trainee nurse, who was forbidden during the war to go into the men's wards, clearly for fear that she could pick up some talk about the war which she might pass on to the enemy.

Most of my colleagues among the workforce were British skilled workers who were more valuable producing war material than serving in the armed forces. My work, which lasted only a few months – circumstances made a return to my firm imperative; it was a 'reserved occupation' anyway – gave me a number of interesting insights. It was for me, and no doubt many fellow refugees in a similar position, the first and only time that I came into direct daily contact with the British working man and woman. I believe it helped me to learn first hand something about the problem of 'class', its nature, effects and much else. But perhaps more significantly, it made me think about whether, and if so how, this subject affected the refugee community as a whole. I think it is worthwhile, in a later chapter in this book, to comment in some detail on this subject, not only as regards my own experiences and feelings, but – more importantly – the conclusions I drew from them, rightly or wrongly, about the status of refugees generally.

My relationships with my colleagues were friendly. I never experienced any anti-Jewish remark or bias. Except for the above-mentioned encounter with my foreman, there was no anti-German-refugee sentiment. That I got on so well with my workmates was perhaps an indication of the way in which we German Jews are able to assimilate. But I certainly noticed differences, to which I shall refer in a separate chapter.

V

Apart from the factors described earlier, I think it is true to say that we experienced the war by and large in the same way as any British citizen. And it is worth repeating that, with few exceptions, we were not treated differently. I even remember an occasion where almost the opposite was the case, though I am not certain whether by accident or design: Dunkirk. Many of our friends were in the Pioneer Corps, some sections of which had been sent overseas. As we all knew, it was not too far-fetched to assume that ex-German Jewish refugees in the army would be in greater danger than British soldiers if they fell into German hands. When the front in France collapsed, we were therefore understandably very worried about the refugee members of the corps. I still remember the relief when we received the telephone call from the wife of a friend of ours in the pioneers who reported that his unit had safely arrived back, being among the first to be evacuated. It was not only relief about the fate of our friends, but also genuine admiration of this caring attitude on the part of the Army during one of the, if not *the*, greatest crises the British nation had ever had to endure.

I had a similar experience on the day Holland was overrun by the Germans. My parents were living there at the time and I spent the day trying to get them out. An influential friend eventually managed to contact the British embassy in the Hague who promised to evacuate them together with the Vic Wells Ballet at that time touring the country. But of course my parents, not realising this and not being British, never thought of contacting the embassy and had to remain in Holland. But it is another indication of how, even during the greatest stress, neither British citizens nor the authorities lost their nerve but were happy to help in individual cases where they could.

Like everybody else, we were immensely fortified whenever we heard a broadcast by Churchill. We all venerated the Royal Family and during the King's Christmas broadcasts, a tradition that was never interrupted, we listened on the wireless, ardently and almost breathlessly willing him to overcome his speech impediment and get the words out. His speeches were usually designed to make this as easy for him as possible, but it was still a traumatic experience for speaker and audience alike. If we did not admire the Queen sufficiently for the way she gave him moral support, it was because we did not realise how much she did without ever seeking the limelight. Today's generations, who love the Queen Mum as the frail centenarian she is and regard her more as a national pet whose human weaknesses are accepted with affection, cannot have any inkling of the important function this strong, brave woman fulfilled when it mattered most.

We listened every Sunday before the 9 o'clock news to the sometimes strange-sounding potpourri of national anthems of every allied nation, most of them at the time overrun by the Germans. This performance was not inappropriately baptised by the people 'The Beggars Opera'. And we looked forward with eager anticipation to the epilogue by JB Priestley every Sunday after the news, until – if the story circulating at the time is to be believed – Churchill apparently considered that Priestley hogged too much of the limelight and ordered the talks to be stopped. If true, it shows that even the greatest of men have their flaws and weaknesses.

For those who lived through the war, the 9 o'clock news always kept its special significance. It was the bulletin that gave the most comprehensive review of the war's progress – as far as the authorities considered it wise to let us hear it. I remember a two-part cartoon in Punch showing in the first picture a radio console in an entirely empty room at 8.59 and in the second the words coming from the loudspeaker 'This is the 9 o'clock news' with the room suddenly filled to overflowing by listeners. I believe that the BBC's decision to move the evening news to 10pm, however reasonably this may have been intended, will leave civilian survivors of the war with a vague sense of deprivation, even though most of them might no longer realise why.

The newscasters, who invariably had to mention their names at the beginning of any news broadcast ('... and this is XYZ reading it') were as well-known and celebrated as today's most prominent pop and football stars. I am not certain whether sufficient official tribute has been paid to some of the actors and comedians who stayed in Britain through the Blitz and whose radio broadcasts (there was no TV) were a definite factor in keeping up our spirits. I still have a distinct feeling of injustice when I remember that Tommy Handley, the best-loved of them, who was undoubtedly a factor in maintaining civilian morale, did not receive a knighthood. And those who heard them will remember with equal affection people like Arthur Askey, Vic Oliver, Bebe Daniels and Ben Lyon, the latter two braving the war here to entertain us, instead of getting back to the safety of America, a country of which they were citizens.

Cultural life went on, not of course at the same volume as before the war but appreciated all the more for that. As far as I remember, the lunchtime concerts at the National Gallery, organised by Myra Hess, were invariably filled to overflowing, not least by army personnel on leave.

We all did our share of fire-watching, though not very seriously unless a raid was imminent or in progress. We lived at the time in a block of flats and I remember my embarrassment when one evening, while I was 'on duty', a fire engine drew up. I had no idea that a small fire had broken out in one of the flats in my block, nor had anyone found it necessary to alert me.

We felt great sympathy for the young British men who had to suffer the unfair competition of American soldiers. These 'GIs' with their abundance of silk stockings, chocolate and – yes! – cigarettes were easily able to lure British girls. Their glamour persuaded not a few young women to marry American servicemen only to find, on arrival in the USA after the war, that some of them were in fact a very unglamorous lot and often dubious characters to boot. Quite a few returned to England and sued for divorce, hence the famous definition of an unsuccessful salesman coined by Tommy Handley: 'He couldn't even sell a return ticket to a GI bride.'

Apart from this, the American army had an important influence on the careers of some refugee musicians. Some managed, on account of their skills, to find work in one of the American Army Bands. Having been officially made American soldiers, they were automatically naturalised and received additional pay – 'for service abroad', although they had never so far set foot in the United States. It was rather different from their treatment in the UK, where even two active RAF fighter pilots of my acquaintance had to remain German (and were promptly nicknamed 'Heini' by their comrades).

One thing is certain - war has a distinct influence on the attitudes and priorities of people in the most diverse respects. One enterprising Lloyd's syndicate issued, at the height of the Blitz, a cover for civilians against being killed in an air raid – the famous 1000:1 insurance, which was taken up by a large number of my clients. Two years on, one of them decided not to renew it. His reason: he had had 'no benefit' from it. All I could do was to send him a letter of congratulation.

When the Queen's Hall, at the time the most famous London concert hall, was destroyed during the first days of the Blitz, most members of a prominent London symphony orchestra, clients of mine, lost their instruments, some of them quite valuable. War damage was not insurable at that time, but a few days later the Government brought out its official scheme whereby losses caused by war risks were covered and the cover was backdated to the beginning of the war. Highly pleased, I advised the members of the orchestra of the good news and sent them claim forms. Quite a few of them did not bother to send them back; I shall never understand why. As I said, war creates strange reactions.

But the most profound change was the attitude towards the life and death of our enemies. Churchill's dictum 'The only good German is a dead German' was quoted with general approval. Not exactly a very delicate remark, but fair enough – this is how we felt at the time. Quite a few years after the war I happened to be sitting in my dentist's waiting room when I came across some very old Punch issues, dating from the war. Idly leafing through one, I saw a cartoon I recognised: a

German airman falling to his death at the end of a parachute full of holes, obviously put there by saboteur slave workers. I don't remember the caption but I do recall that at the time, I found it quite funny. Of course, during the war they had wanted to kill us and we them, but fancy considering a cartoon showing someone falling to his death a joke! It made me realise that war brings out in us the best in the shape of heroism and selflessness as well as the worst in the shape of mindless cruelty and 'jokes' in the worst possible taste. Is it too much to hope that this will never again be put to the test? Sadly, almost certainly, yes, it is too much.

Relations with Germans and Germany after the war

I

During the mid-1970s a German concert impresario asked me whether I would do him the favour of writing to the famous violinist Isaac Stern, whom I had the privilege to know slightly. Stern had decided never again to appear professionally in Germany. Would I try to make him change his mind? I replied that I did not regard it as my function to do anything towards persuading Jews to forgive Germany. However, thinking about it, I became intrigued by the question not only of our own attitude towards Germany but also that of people, prominent or otherwise, who had not been Jews or refugees in the first place. This had been a very live issue at the beginning of the Nazi period (vide the famous letter from Bronislav Huberman, in which he took Wilhelm Furtwängler to task for staying in Germany). I therefore decided to write to Isaac Stern after all, and did so in a deliberately challenging way in order to elicit a clear reply.

Accordingly, I pointed out to him that no German born after 1930 could actually have made a reasoned decision to become a Nazi and that a considerable number of people of the older generation were obviously no longer alive, having died either during the war or through natural causes. In addition there had been quite a few anti-Nazis in Germany. Hence, I concluded, no more than 20 per cent of the German population could be former Nazis and presumably no greater percentage of anti-Semites were alive in Germany. 'Name me,' I concluded, 'one country in the world where anti-Semites make up fewer than 20 per cent of its population. If you were only to perform in countries where there are fewer than that percentage, I am afraid your field of activities would be very limited if not almost non-existent.'

Stern replied that my argument was quite logical, but not sufficiently strong to make him change his mind. Germany was for obvious reasons a special case to which reasoned thought did not apply, especially by Jews. And, of course, he was right. Moreover, some time later I was told that his wife had lost several near relatives during the Holocaust. However, the story has an intriguing sequel: since then Isaac Stern has agreed to hold master classes in Germany. I consider this highly significant. It seems that there comes a point when we all have to take a fresh look at old problems, previous experiences and memories, however painful they may be. How long can you go on boycotting a country because of its past? Pablo Casals did, as far as I know, spurning Spain all his life. But his reason was also its political situation after peace had been restored after the civil war. Even so, I think it is safe to say that he was the exception rather than the rule. And as for the attitude of politicians all over the world, I'd rather not comment!

One thing seems clear: the attitude towards Germany shown by former refugees cannot possibly be uniform. Apart from more or less strongly held personal convictions, there must be a great many cases where the motivation stems from personal experience rather than general principles. If you personally suffered physical hardship and persecution, or if close members of your family perished in the Holocaust, your attitude is almost bound to be different from that of people who were fortunate enough to be spared any such tragedy. In theory, there is no objective reason why this should be so. A country whose citizens committed these unspeakable crimes against members of our race should be shunned for ever and a day, irrespective of our personal involvement. In practice, however, there is little doubt that human nature does not work that way, but reacts quite differently. If there is a war in a distant country and we read in the papers that 1000 innocent civilians were killed or maimed in an air raid, our reaction (provided, of course, we don't belong to one of the organisations that make it their specific task to deal actively with tragedies and injustices of this kind) will certainly be disgust at this crime against humanity, compassion with the victims and, hopefully, a desire to help through a charitable donation.

But these are emotions of, for want of a better word, a 'general' kind. If we were to hear on the same day that one of our neighbours, with whom we had been on no more than greeting terms, had been severely injured or even killed in a traffic accident (which, as it turned out, was nobody's fault, so that there is no-one against whom to direct our wrath) I offer no prizes for the answer to the question which of the two events would affect us more. It is usually not the severity of an event or even the circumstances surrounding it which are of primary importance to us, but the degree of its closeness to ourselves. Whether we like it or not, there seems to be no reason why the same should not apply to the long-term development of our relationship with Germany and the Germans. We may not agree with it, we may even greatly dislike it, but this is what experience shows.

II

While this book is not a memoir, I think I should explain where I stand myself in this matter. Both my wife and I were able to leave Germany before the full horror of the regime had manifested itself and, thankfully, all our near relatives escaped the Holocaust. But for me there is an additional factor. A mentally handicapped brother of mine had, since his early youth, been looked after as an inmate of a famous German institution run by a Christian charity (Bethel, founded by Pastor von Bodelschwingh). When my parents emigrated, they decided that it would be better for him not to be uprooted but to remain where he had been staying for so many years. Of course, they made ample financial provision so as to guarantee the means for his upkeep, as they thought, indefinitely. It was undoubtedly the right decision in the light of circumstances known to them at the time, and when the Nazis' Euthanasia programme got under way, it was too late to try and rescue him.

The Bethel Institution reacted superbly. It succeeded in protecting every one of its many charges, its managing head preferring a prison sentence to abandoning his patients. When after the war various parts of Germany were occupied and run by the Allies separately, and no money could be transferred from one zone to another – my brother lived in the British, the money was in the French zone – the Institution kept him without worrying whether it would ever receive a penny. After we had regained contact, it became clear that my brother had not only survived the war unscathed but was in excellent physical condition; and his mental state showed clearly that he had been protected from the stresses and traumas to which Jews had been exposed in Germany during that period. In other words, immediately after the war I received at first-hand the fullest possible proof that the existence of 'good Germans' was not a myth, but that there had been quite a number who had genuinely been in that category. It was inevitable that this should colour my opinions to quite some extent.

But for at least a decade or so after the war this did not affect my or anyone else's attitude towards Germany in practice. For instance, my father had written his memoirs in German. This book has, as it happens, become an important source work for the study of violin and general music history during the last ten years of the 19th and the first 40 years of the 20th century but when, shortly after the war, I tried to publish it posthumously, it was for a considerable time quite impossible to find a British or American publisher prepared to accept it. One of the reasons was that it would have had to be translated into English first, and also edited in certain respects. The idea – and this is the point I want to make – of having it published in the original language in Germany simply did not occur to me or anyone else whose advice I sought, although it would have been perfectly logical at least to consider it. Germany was simply non-existent as a normal partner for anything whatever; it had become a 'non-country'.

III

Things tended to change when Germany began to recover and in particular when the possibility of restitution for German Jewish refugees slowly turned from a distant possibility into reality. I am not saying by any means that the fact of our receiving compensation payments was the reason for this change of mind. On the contrary, our firm opinion had always been (and still is) that all those who have suffered are fully entitled to substantial compensation, however great the cost to Germany. A few people who had vowed never again to have anything whatever to do with Germany stuck to their principles and refused even to apply for restitution. One has to admire this high-minded attitude of allowing a moral viewpoint to override practical considerations, but I can't say that I agree with it. However base the crime, there is no reason why one should refuse compensation from its perpetrators, always bearing in mind that in our case no amount of money can be regarded as sufficient to wipe out the guilt. It is not surprising that the overwhelming majority of refugees were of the same practical turn of mind and, indeed, for many restitution was a means of considerably improving their situation, in a number of cases even saving them from destitution. I am not trying to belittle in any way the motives of those who did not apply, but I daresay that very few, if any, were in that dire financial situation.

There were cases where the pendulum swung the opposite way: German restitution payments in the form of pensions were initially subject to British income tax. It took a great many years and considerable effort before the Inland Revenue could be persuaded to adopt the correct point of view and regard these payments not as income but as what they were – non-taxable compensation. But at the time when pensions were still taxable, there were several ways of mitigating the position and one method of reversing it completely: for some technical reason too difficult to be grasped by a layman – or at any rate by me – payments became tax-free if you possessed or reverted to German nationality. After the war every refugee who wished to do so was entitled to re-adopt German nationality without, incidentally, giving up British citizenship. Hence by becoming a German national again, one could avoid all the income tax on compensation payments in the form of pensions, sometimes a substantial amount. It never entered my wife's or my head to do so (in fact she declared her intention to divorce me if I ever considered it) and to my knowledge, very few of us refugees made use of this possibility, preferring to forgo the financial advantage this step would bring. However, I do not criticize those who did. It was, after all, nothing but a formality, a technicality without real significance. Yet most of us felt instinctively that, whether or not we resumed relations with Germany, there was a need to keep our distance. Re-adopting German nationality therefore would not do. It was a badge of closeness which very few of us wanted to wear, although 'some of my best friends ...' In the end, it was a matter for individual decision, depending very much on one's own particular views and circumstances. If, for instance, it was a question of getting out of severe financial hardship, only those who have ever experienced it have a right to criticize those who succumbed.

It has to be said that a number of emigrants made exaggerated compensation demands. But I have to confess that practically everybody in our circle – myself included – shared the opinion that the higher the amount achieved, the better. Considering the type and severity of German crimes, no compensation could be high enough, hence nobody condemned those who tried to take advantage. Exaggerated demands were often supported by somewhat elastic reports by medical men, mostly German refugees themselves, appointed by German embassies as independent experts. But some of these referees took their responsibilities more seriously and did their best to assess every claim impartially, not hesitating to indicate instances where they considered them too high or entirely unjustified. I am sorry to have to report that this entirely proper and honourable attitude was not at all welcomed by the refugee community generally, not to mention those directly concerned and I believe it caused some of these doctors to lose a number of patients – something which, in fairness, one has to regard as quite unjustified and regrettable.

I would like to stress again that it was not the compensation payments as such that softened the anti-German attitude on the part of refugees, but rather that they necessitated the resumption of some sort of relationship with Germans, be it tribunals, solicitors or simply the authorities paying the actual compensation – or for that matter fringe benefits such as contribution to medical expenses. In the long run, regular communication with a party in a civilized way is bound to have its effects. Hence even some of those people who had initially sworn under no circumstances to be in touch with, let alone set foot inside Germany ever again, gradually abandoned this hard line. A number of emigrants had actually gone back to live in Germany, which entailed in many cases an attractive resettlement allowance. Again, I don't think anybody has a right to criticize them. Some immigrants just could not get used to living in a foreign country, were quite lost and unable to earn a living. For them, going back was a life-saver.

There was one category of people who went back for

other reasons: former communists who were only too eager to enter the East German paradise. I did not happen to be in personal contact with any such 'returnees' but I believe the result did not always come up to expectations.

IV

Disregarding the extreme cases at both ends of the scale, the question of whether and to what degree to re-establish connections with Germany was one that everybody had to solve in accordance with his own conscience. I freely admit that I decided in favour of it. When, in 1980, I retired from my original firm, I did not want to give up work for personal as well as financial reasons so I accepted a position in a large firm of Lloyd's brokers interested in extending their German connections. This entailed frequent business contacts with Germans and travel to Germany, much of which I could not help but enjoy.

Of course I had reservations. Though, after the war, it was difficult to find a German who would admit to having been a National Socialist (as the black joke goes there had originally been 40 million Jews in Germany – every adult German claimed to have saved the life of at least *one*), there was yet a real possibility, even after a few decades, of encountering a former Nazi or Nazi sympathizer, and this risk was still ever-present in my mind. As it turned out, it remained a thought. The people I dealt with, mostly insurance company officials or heads of broking firms, were usually in the 30-50 age group, ie mostly too young to have been party members of their own volition. Nevertheless, I was wary. A typical first meeting would go like this: after five minutes' talk my host would invariably remark, 'I must congratulate you on your linguistic talents. Where did you learn such perfect German?' To which my equally invariable reply was: 'In Germany, until, as a Jew, I was forced to emigrate.' I then waited for any adverse reaction – voluntary or involuntary – which would have put an end to any further conversation. It never came. In the course of years I established many good personal contacts and, in a few cases, real friendships.

A slightly different problem arose when you met people with whom you had been friendly at school or university. In those cases, especially at a few school reunions I attended, I could not always bring myself to delve too closely into the antecedents of my former mates, but instead decided to give them the benefit of the doubt. They had been punished enough as it was. Not the 'politically correct' attitude, no doubt, but who can be strong and principled all the time? The same applied when you met Germans on holiday and were the recipient of friendly overtures, except in cases where the Nazi connection appeared obvious. It is – for me at any rate – anything but easy to repulse friendly approaches made on a social level, and so I may well have been superficially, and of course unknowingly, friendly with former Nazis or Nazi sympathizers. The main thing was never to leave the other party in doubt about my own origins – a general Jewish trait to which I refer elsewhere.

I often wondered what my German opposite numbers thought about us. After all, irrespective of any question of war guilt, the Allied bombing raids had been infinitely worse than anything the Germans had done to us during the first years of the war and must have been regarded by German civilians as nothing short of barbaric. I confess that it was a subject I avoided – whether out of tact or lack of moral courage I dare not decide. However, it seemed that the average German understood that whatever had happened to his country bore no comparison to Nazi crimes and I noticed surprisingly little rancour.

I once received an indirect indication of this. During a lunch with a group of Germans following a prolonged business session, one acquaintance asked me straight out: 'We are getting on so well together. You obviously like being in Germany, why don't you move back?'

I felt this demanded a frank answer: 'Yes, I do enjoy it here, and I have made friends. But these are visits. It would be quite unthinkable for me to live permanently amongst people who perpetrated the atrocities upon members of my race which the Germans committed. This is a gut feeling which has no relation to individual friendships.' I don't know – nor did I care – how this went down. There were a few dissenting voices – 'We are not the same people' etc – but I was able to point to a parallel. During that same luncheon one of my hosts, who during the war had been the youngest member of a German U-boat crew, had told us that, after several decades of peace, he still broke into a cold sweat every morning on hearing his alarm clock go off; it reminded him of the alarm bell on his boat that indicated an emergency.

I made the obvious comment: 'You clearly and consciously know that your fears are completely groundless but you can nevertheless not overcome this automatic feeling of panic. The impression it made on you at the time is indelible. My attitude towards the impossibility of returning to Germany is of a similar kind – not supported by reason but by instinct and impossible to overcome.'

This explanation was accepted as convincing, which indeed it was. There comes a point at which even the 'passage of time' ceases to have validity.

V

So, if no former Nazis were to be found in Germany, if they had all at heart been against the regime, the obvious question was: why hadn't they done anything about it? The German resistance had been, with a few outstanding and heroic exceptions, very ineffective. Was this not an indication that there had been very few 'good Germans' about? If there had been more, what excuse did they have for their inactivity? Justified questions indeed, which I think we should look at objectively. 'Objectively' is the operative word. In case any reader should still think that this is an exercise to try and find excuses or even reasons to condone what happened, let me paraphrase the famous saying from the TV sit-com "Allo, 'allo': 'Listen carefully. I shall say it only once' (more): National Socialism and what it did was the most horrendous crime of the 20th century. But even this is no reason why we should not look at some aspects of it that are not always given full attention.

The German Holocaust and what went on before it under the Nazis were the worst crimes because they were unequalled in viciousness, cynicism combined with organisational skill, and focus. But man's inhumanity to man is nothing new. Leaving aside wars, in the last 2000 years we have had, to name but a few atrocities, the horrifying treatment of slave gladiators and Christians in the Roman Empire; the burning of heretics and witches at the stake in the Middle Ages; the guillotines of the French Revolution; the Russian pogroms; the lynch parties in the USA; public executions in Great Britain. All are horrific – yet all were greatly enjoyed by a considerable part of the population at the time. And, in a way, all have been 'forgiven' by later generations in the sense that they have become 'history'. We learned about the Romans, the French Revolution, the Middle Ages et al at school, but I cannot remember any twinges of revulsion on my part or that of my classmates, let alone teachers. I have plenty of acquaintances who for one reason or another dislike Italians, Frenchmen, Russians or Americans, but I cannot recall a single one who has ever given the misdeeds I have just mentioned as the reason. And don't we all today use expressions like 'thumbs down' without giving a thought to the fact that at one time this meant the random decision by a frenzied mob over life or death for some unfortunate gladiator?

We Jews are worried about future generations forgetting what happened between 1939 and 1945 or even falling for the wiles of the Holocaust deniers. I think there is little danger of that: the events, thanks to books of memoirs, testimonials by eyewitnesses, permanent memorials, Holocaust museums and enterprises such as the Shoah Foundation, are too well documented for this to happen. But what is far more likely, judging by the experience in countless similar cases, is that these events will become 'history' and be discussed as such more or less dispassionately with moral judgments, if any, taking a back seat in most cases.

This will not happen in our lifetime, and I am glad of it. But there are straws in the wind. Not a few co-refugees with whom I have discussed such matters have expressed surprise that their grandchildren seem in a way more interested than their children in what happened to them; not due to lack of love or compassion on their children's part but, I believe, on account of what I will call lack of distance from the events which apparently makes it difficult for the generation immediately following ours to come to terms with our experiences – an unpalatable phenomenon whose existence it is as well to recognise, even though trying to find answers to the questions arising from it is way beyond the scope of this book, let alone my own understanding.

We encounter the same difficulty if we try to find the reasons why Hitler came to power. As a politically aware student in Germany I was able to observe the rise of National Socialism. If you ask me to explain what happened and why and how, you won't be able to stop me for the next hour. I can cite a dozen facts and reasons but I am afraid they do not go to the heart of the matter. There must be an element in these cases that leads to some sort of spontaneous (or for that matter non-spontaneous) combustion. We know it is there, but unfortunately no-one has as yet been able to identify it.

What seems clear is that any such movement must hang its hat on some politically correct pronouncement which even its opponents have to agree with. In the Nazis' case it was the Treaty of Versailles, the red rag for every German which enabled them to get a foothold by obtaining the partial blessing or at least approval of a substantial part of the population. In most cases of mass hysteria the masses have been conditioned by propaganda, surprisingly no less powerful in former times than that exerted by the media today. But propaganda does not necessarily always play a part, and an overpowering popular emotion need not invariably result in evil. The best modern example is the tragic death of Princess Diana, the popular reaction to which, however heartfelt, is now widely recognised as having been out of all proportion. We have only to compare it, for instance, to the genuine but measured mourning displayed at the almost simultaneous passing of Mother Theresa who had done the same type of good deeds as Diana but for a period more than three times as long.

But whether for good or evil, there can be popular reactions whose origin is obscure, which can be self-perpetuating and whose strength and consequences cannot easily be foreseen. We must hope that a discovery of the reasons and the devising of counter measures will not be too long delayed so as to prevent further catastrophes for humanity.

Now let us turn to a further point which I have already briefly referred to. If there were indeed so many opponents to the Nazi regime, how come they did not express their opposition openly but let things happen? Let us consider a different scenario. Imagine at the time of Princess Diana's accident you had been with a large party, all of them ardent Princess Diana sympathizers and strongly opposed to the treatment she was said to have received from the Royal Family; but you had been of a different opinion, namely that it was feasible to apportion blame to both sides. Or take the case of the terrible murder of a little girl by a paedophile, resulting in justified revulsion against those people, shared by all those present except you, who happened to feel that the expression of this disgust, whipped up by part of the press, was indiscriminate and way over the top. Are you quite certain that, being in a minority of one vis-à-vis the passionately-held opinions of all the others, you would have raised your voice and braved the inevitable hostility? I am sure that those who can honestly answer 'yes' will be very few. I wouldn't have done so. Why stick my neck out? For what?

Now translate this into the situation during the Nazi period when even mild doubts, let alone frankly expressed opposition, could be positively dangerous to life and limb, freedom and employment of oneself and one's family. Wouldn't most of us have preferred to keep as quiet as possible? Of course, this was wrong in principle. There were some who did speak up in public; and look what happened to the great majority of them!

I have already mentioned elsewhere that not a few English Jews informed us German Jewish refugees that our fate had, to some extent, been our own fault – assimilation instead of emphasizing our Jewishness. All of us who were living in Germany know how ludicrous this opinion is. In some situations it is best to keep as low a profile as you can but there is no reason why this should not also apply to the average gentile opponent of the Nazi regime. As for myself, all I can say is that I am glad I am a Jew and never had to face this moral dilemma.

And let us not confuse genuine German nationalism with National Socialism. One illustrative example of the former was the famous German conductor Wilhelm Furtwängler whom I have already mentioned. He was an ardent German but certainly not a Nazi, let alone an anti-Semite – as I happen to know from my family's personal experience. Yet he stayed in Germany and, at least in public, kept his opinions to himself. He could easily have defected on one of his foreign concert tours and have reaped both genuine moral acclaim by the outside world and financial advantages for himself, but he didn't. The condemnation he received from many people was certainly unjustified. There were undoubtedly many cases like his. You cannot blame people for not being heroic. This does not excuse in any way whatever the Nazis' crimes and those who condoned them, but perhaps it is putting the attitude of many German citizens in perspective.

Public opinion can be very unforgiving for the wrong reasons. I have never understood the case of Rudolf Kastner. I confess I know too little about it to speak with any authority, but surely there is no doubt that his activities saved the lives of several thousand Jews who would otherwise have perished. How he managed this is of secondary importance. He certainly was not a 'collaborator' in the accepted sense, in that he did nothing to further the Nazi cause. His 'crime', if I understand it correctly, was that after the war he spoke up for a high ranking Nazi who had been helping him and with whom for that reason he had tried to be, and in fact had been, on good personal terms. There is a curious, well-documented parallel: occasionally kidnap victims become very friendly with their kidnappers. Understandably, Kastner was a witness in that Nazi's favour, putting forward the mitigating facts as he knew them. If this is a crime, I plead guilty to having done exactly the same: my parents were caught in Holland by the German invasion. For a long time they tried in vain to leave Holland and get permission to go to my father's native Hungary. Eventually, after two years, they succeeded. I happened to know the name of the Nazi official who had made the decision. When I read in the papers that he had been accused of war crimes I wrote to the court citing his one good deed, which I knew of personally. I never received a reply. I don't know how the proceedings against him ended; I have even forgotten his name. But I am glad I acted as I did. Justice has to be impartial.

VI

For some refugees who returned to Germany, things turned out badly. A married couple, good friends of ours, decided to enter a German old age 'colony' which on the face of it was very attractive. We all tried to dissuade them from their folly, putting forward the obvious reasons, but to no avail. 'We have a few old friends there and can keep ourselves isolated from the rest. Moreover, the place is very near the Swiss border. In case matters should become oppressive, we could always obtain temporary relief by jumping into the car and being with our Swiss friends in no time.' I am sorry to say that after the husband's death the widow found that most of her old friends had died too and, in view of the couple's previous negative attitude, there were insufficient contacts to replace them. You cannot live for good in a country whose citizens you do not have some sort of empathy with, even if you are initially of the misguided opinion that this is desirable or feasible. Tragically, this case ended in the widow's suicide.

At the other end of the scale, several people who went on a visit to Germany did not want it to be known that they had originally been German themselves, presumably to avoid the risk of any kind of friendly contact with the natives or simply to make it clear that they were citizens of another country. So as not to be recognised as former Germans, they decided not to speak a word of German but to stick strictly to English. Needless to say this strategy hardly ever worked. What they did not appear to realise was that in most cases, the moment they opened their mouths it became abundantly clear even to the most unobservant German that they were not original Britons. They must have frequently been the cause of silent German mirth and gossip, which I think is the last thing you need as a former refugee visiting Germany.

I believe I am right in saying that the days immediately before their first visit to Germany were an anxious time for most refugees. They certainly were for me. We had, after all, left under traumatic circumstances; would it not all be too much for us emotionally? Would our feelings become unduly hostile or, the opposite, too nostalgic and would we, God forbid, even have an urge to return permanently? In most cases we need not have worried. I think the majority of us considered ourselves as Britons re-visiting a foreign country. (Austrians visiting Vienna may have been the exception!) Our manners and attitudes had become British; we had forgotten German ways.

I remember on my very first visit having an argument with a rather obtuse counter clerk in a bank. Eventually I lost my temper and began to shout at him.. Even as I was doing this, I was asking myself in an almost horrified way: 'How on earth can you behave so badly! And this man's reaction will be highly embarrassing for me! Serves me right!' But to my surprise, he visibly backed down and did as he was told. I had forgotten that in former times – I think it has changed now – shouting was the German way of getting what you wanted. And I still recall my astonishment when, after a concert in Berlin, I was queuing – or so I thought – at the cloakroom to retrieve my coat, and everybody was rudely pushing forward to be served first. You had to play it the same way if you wanted to get anywhere. It was only then that I remembered the practically inevitable 'cloakroom battles' ('Garderobeschlachten') of my youth on these occasions. Queues were practically unknown in Germany as soon as rationing ended a few years after the war. Even the German expression for it has a slightly offensive overtone – 'anstehen', to stand in line.

Something else I had forgotten was the German romanticism which, at least initially, survived the last war. I remember a former classmate of mine, a girl with whom I had been violently in love – unsuccessfully, I regret to say – and whom I met again after many years while visiting her home town on business. At the end of my stay I was leaving Germany for home and, after counting the remnants of my German money, I decided on a gentlemanly gesture. 'Here,' I said to the hotel porter, 'take these 12 Marks, keep four as a tip for yourself, buy as many roses as you can for the remaining eight Marks and have them sent to such-and-such an address.' (The amounts mentioned show that this was a very long time ago indeed!) I received an enthusiastic letter of thanks: 'How attentive of you to send me the same number of roses as the number of years since we first met!' I doubt that this could have happened anywhere else, and I did not rob her of her illusion.

What about gentile Germans who are resident in this country? I happen to know very few and with those I do I am, with very few exceptions, only on terms of superficial acquaintance. Presumably they have as little interest in me as I have in them. They are obviously here by their own choice and accept the British way of life, at least temporarily, hence the question of their antecedents does not normally arise. Many of them probably do not even understand that, for refugees, there is a problem. I remember a case shortly after the war when a German applied for a job in my company. He had been a prisoner of war in this country, married an English girl and stayed on. I told him that, with a clientele which at that time consisted to a large extent of German Jewish refugees, I could not possibly employ him. He seemed surprised and could not understand why: 'In Germany I had nothing against Jews. In fact I was always on friendly terms with them until they were taken away.' Exactly.

So, how to sum up our attitude towards Germany, as I think it is and should be developing? I can do no better than quote the concluding passages of an article written some time ago by the well-known writer and musicologist Norman Lebrecht: 'Not to forget, which would be unforgivable; nor even to forgive, which is a divine prerogative. But to found a new relationship with modern Germany, a multinational, multicultural society like our own, in which the past is a foreign country and the future will nourish a revivified Jewish community.'

In particular ...

The vast majority of refugees (I am disregarding the comparatively few who came from other countries *after* the last war) arrived here prior to September 1939, some at almost the last moment, in that case usually not direct from Germany, where emigration during the last months before the war became so difficult as to be almost impossible. So, by the time war broke out, some of us had been in this country for over six and the majority for two to four years. I do not believe that the situations of those who came early and those who came late are by now, as I write this, very different – in this respect the war was a great leveller. On the other hand it is interesting to speculate whether there was any marked difference between the position of refugees during the pre- and post-war periods..

Outwardly, undoubtedly. During the war we immigrants had been through traumatic experiences mostly similar to those of the British people themselves. In part they had been identical – the Blitz, the constantly changing war situation, the fear of invasion. In other respects, there had been differences either way. We obviously had fewer friends and family members on active service, but on the other hand many of us had relatives in Germany or German-dominated territories whose fates caused us the utmost anxiety, unfortunately, as it turned out in a great many cases, with very good reason. We had more to fear from a German invasion, let alone victory, than our British gentile – and possibly, at least initially, even Jewish – contemporaries. But these varying factors had not affected the general shared experience, nor our contribution to the war effort in the ways open to us. In consequence, our position had undoubtedly greatly improved. Practically none of us were any longer subject to restrictions regarding work and residence and we were therefore able to take our rightful place in society. More and more of us were being or had been naturalised. We had got used to British ways and understood some of the strange customs and traditions – as far as they had not radically altered or even entirely disappeared during the war years – that had so puzzled us when we had first arrived. And I believe – equally important – the British, in their own way, had got used to us..

So, at first glance, it would have seemed logical to divide this part of the book into the pre-war and the post-war period. But on thinking about it, I came to the conclusion that this was not the right way to look at it. The change in our situation notwithstanding, the division would have been somewhat artificial. For the remarkable and somewhat surprising fact is that, at least as I see it, the passage of time, though it affected matters a great deal outwardly, has altered comparatively little below the surface. I think therefore I am right in saying that, external factors apart, the basic difference between our pre- and post-war status is far less marked than one might have expected. In this respect the years 1939-45 cannot be regarded as a watershed. In this chapter, I am therefore making no division between the time before and after the war.

What are the reasons for the relatively small differences? Hadn't we, through the passage of time, become ever more 'British'? Undoubtedly, being the born 'assimilators' we are, we had already substantially identified with Great Britain and its problems – had begun to feel British – at quite an early stage of our stay. A good illustration of this is, I think, the important role we attributed to the British Monarchy and as a consequence, the way in which the abdication crisis of 1937 affected us.

Refugees and the Monarchy

Few of the younger generation can have any inkling of how much times have changed as far as freedom of the press is concerned. Pre-war, there was an unwritten law that it was just not on for anything out of the ordinary, let alone unfavourable, about the Royal Family to appear in the papers unless it had been approved by their press office beforehand, tacitly or otherwise. The relationship between the as yet uncrowned King Edward VIII and Mrs Simpson had been long-standing. Just think what the tabloids would have made of it today from its very beginning! But nothing whatsoever had appeared in the British press except possibly coded hints that could be understood only by a few insiders, such as, for instance, placing photographs, innocent in themselves, in juxtaposition. So the remarkable fact remained that there was really nothing apt to alert the British population, including most of us refugees, to the crisis that was brewing up, much less prepare them for it. It is not impossible that this general unawareness was helped by the attitude that nobody *wanted* to know anything that might be damaging to the Royal Family and in consequence we closed our eyes to it.

This changed in one fell swoop when the Bishop of Bradford drew attention to the situation in a very outspoken sermon criticising the King. True, there had already been quite a few reports in foreign papers which were read more frequently by refugees than British citizens, but those who knew more took surprisingly little notice and the matter was rarely discussed. It seems that we were already subscribing to the view that at that time foreign reports were highly suspect and unreliable compared with what appeared in the British press. We were all taken by surprise when the facts came out. And, judging by my own feelings and those of many friends with whom I endlessly discussed the matter, it is no exaggeration to say that refugees as a body reacted to events by and large in the same way as most of the British population: we were deeply affected and greatly worried by it.

It would be interesting to know whether a larger proportion of the refugee community took a more liberal view of the King's behaviour than the British citizens, but I don't think any statistics exist. However, it did not really matter what one thought about the rights and wrongs of the affair. Opinions on whether or not the King was acting in accordance with his duty and station, and particularly whether or not, and if so in what form, he should marry Mrs Simpson, were fiercely divided, with the result that, whatever stance you took, you were bound to be at one with a substantial section of the British people and opposed to another equally large one. Should the head of the Royal family take a commoner as his spouse? Could she be Queen? At that time we – everybody – lacked the insight and practical experience we have since gained (at considerable expense to the monarchy) regarding the desirability (or otherwise) and the possible consequences of accepting non-Royals into the Royal family. Opinions were therefore based more on gut reaction and surmise than on actual knowledge.

Should – could – there be a morganatic marriage? And, a quaint question equally important in the eyes of the Church and therefore at that time in many people's: should a member of the Royal family marry a divorced person '*with the previous spouse still being alive*'? The importance attributed to this latter point was of course evidenced many years later by Princess Margaret's decision not to marry a man in a similar position; her life might well have taken an entirely different – and perhaps happier – course if morals and opinions at that time had been as liberal as they are today. I believe that opinions held by refugees on this particular point differed from those of many British people. So we may be said to have been somewhat ahead of our times in this instance.

When the King did abdicate, we, like quite a few British people, thought the end of the monarchy was a distinct possibility and shared the deep general dismay and unhappiness. For, as I have already mentioned, most of us were greatly impressed by the British monarchy and readily accepted that members of the Royal Family were 'special'. Today, as we all know, more and more people, not only in the Commonwealth but also in Britain itself, consider the monarchy and the system of privilege that goes with it to be out of date, snobbish, undesirable and ripe for abolition. I have little doubt that life and experiences in Germany at the time would have disabused most of these protagonists of their opinion.

The refugees' stance on monarchy is not without interest. After all, most of us had grown up in a republic following the German Kaiser's forced abdication after the First World War. In our homeland, therefore, most of us had been anti-monarchists. Though many of our teachers weren't and we therefore regarded them with some suspicion, we were taught at school to believe in 'Republic', not 'Monarchy'. How come, then, that many of us changed our minds so readily and did not even realise the apparent contradiction between our previous and present attitudes?

Apart from the obvious fact that, in the face of the Hitler regime, we would have accepted any non-Nazi form of state with open arms, the difference lies no doubt in the character of the former German as opposed to the British monarchy. Of course, many of the younger refugees had had no direct experience of the German institution. Like the British, it had been a constitutional monarchy but in some respects more in name than in practice. The German Kaiser and his family were regarded as entirely above criticism by the common man. I have already referred to the specific offence of *lèse majesté* (*Majestätsbeleidigung*) which could lead to prison sentences for those found guilty of it. If such a law were to exist in this country today, it is unlikely that editors of any tabloid would ever be out of prison. More important, though, the Kaiser had had a far greater political say than the British King or Queen. Personally I believe that, whether we consciously realised it or not, this, for us, was the crux of the matter. Monarchy as it exists in this country is, for many of us who have gone through so many different experiences, the ideal form of government. What is it that makes it so attractive? The reasons as I see them may not appeal to monarchists, but let me briefly digress and look at them, for, as I said, I believe they influenced us refugees subconsciously.

There can be no doubt that the monarchic state form

is highly elitist and undoubtedly perpetuates the class system. But as I discuss elsewhere in this book, I regard a really classless society as an impossibility. In addition, it is an indisputable fact that in all human nature there is the need for someone, or even a whole class of supermen or women, who we can look up to and admire or even worship. Nowadays, with the advent of electronics and marketing techniques, these people can be created with the greatest of ease, sometimes almost at the touch of a button. In others, they have real skills, for instance footballers or (far more rarely) pop stars, which does not alter the fact that their importance is usually vastly overrated. Objects of adulation can also be dictators, even though in their case the adulation will more often than not be compulsory. But in former times the main objects were, for the majority of people, members of the monarchy; and I believe, to an important extent they still are. People may deride royalty, but it is amusing to observe them if they happen to come into contact with a Royal personage. Their attitude and demeanour suddenly become unrecognisable. But this is by the way.

If we worship football or pop stars or even politicians, this is our decision, whether misguided or not. But a monarch is not elected and we therefore have no say in the choice of him or her. But both kinds have one thing in common: their basic personal ordinariness. The fact that the reason for their elevated position lies in their feet, the size of their bosom, their contortions on the stage or simply in the accident of their birth does not guarantee that they are superior persons in any other respect. And of course, most of them aren't. Their special talents or position apart, they are as frail and ordinary as the rest of us, sometimes even more so. In nine out of ten cases, the way they appear to their adoring public is based on illusion. What is more, the adulation they receive as demi-gods is bound to affect their character – they begin to believe they are higher beings. If your opinions are always listened to with respect and you are rarely, if ever, seriously contradicted, you inevitably begin to believe you are a special, infallible person, you become a megalomaniac, and you begin to behave accordingly. Hence the catastrophic consequences of a dictatorship.

But with the British Monarchy this does not matter. For while monarchs may temporarily or permanently affect or even dictate tastes, fashion and moral customs, they are in effect not able to exert any influence on matters of real importance in the life of the nation. Hence, this hero worship, addressed as it is to essentially powerless people, is harmless. It does not matter either whether or not they 'deserve' it. There are numerous examples of vicious or inadequate monarchs, but the public were usually kept at a sufficient distance for their blemishes not to become generally noticeable, so they did not interfere with the population's hero worship. It is simply a question of the right PR. One of the main reasons for the monarchy's present troubles is that during the past decades their PR no longer functioned properly, and this was due to the fact that the monarchy consciously tried to lower the barriers and thereby destroyed some of its mystique. But this has nothing to do with the fact that genuinely constitutional monarchs do not have real power.

And this is precisely why the British Monarchy is such an ideal system. Its representatives, our Kings and

Queens, are worshipped, but they have no actual say in the scheme of things. Everything is done in their name, yes, but it is not their own decisions to which they lend their name. If monarchs happen to be great, this is an added bonus, as it were. If they are not, never mind, provided their PR can gloss over their faults. And this, it is worth repeating, presupposes that the public are not allowed too near. One must hope that on this subject royal spin doctors have learnt from their past mistakes.

In brief, hero worship is necessary for us, the people. Never mind that it usually spoils the character of those who are being worshipped. What does it matter, as long as they do not have the power to act in accordance with their exaggerated opinion of themselves? Our powerless demi-gods are comparable to lightning conductors who attract dangerous lightning successfully and make it harmless.

What does this have to do with refugees? Nothing directly because, as I said, we never realised all this consciously. But I believe that subconsciously it contributed to the monarchy giving us the feeling of security and permanency that we had been lacking during the days of the wobbly Weimar Republic with all its controversies and dangerous situations, when you never quite knew where you stood from one day to the next. The British monarchy was, I am convinced, one of the things that made this country so attractive to us. And I think that is why we were affected so much when the crisis broke, although we were not yet British citizens. We were about to be deprived of the sense of permanence and security that had surrounded us since our arrival in this country, even if it had not made us feel more secure about our immediate fate.

There can be little doubt that, like most of the population, we misjudged the real character of King Edward VIII. It had been successfully hidden from us. I shall never forget the breathless attention with which we hung on the undoubtedly very moving parting words of the King's last broadcast. The fact that long negotiations of a practical and financial nature between his advisers and the Government had preceded the abdication was glossed over and conveniently forgotten. It did not fit the picture.

The transition to the new monarch – who was unprepared, without obvious talents and with a speech defect to boot – was unbelievably smooth. The people's affection was transferred to him and his family without question – more proof of how much we need a symbol we can look up to. With the benefit of hindsight we now know that if Edward VIII had remained King, considering the admiration he and Mrs Simpson expressed for Hitler, the course of later events might well have been very different. For, although the King did not have the real power of political decision, he could still influence the climate of opinion in the country, which would very likely have been the opposite of what it actually became once Churchill succeeded to the post of prime minister. It is, incidentally, worth recalling that Churchill, while still out of office, was one of the people strenuously looking for ways that would make abdication unnecessary. It shows once again that even the most outstanding people with the most intimate inside knowledge do not always judge matters correctly. As far as we Jews are concerned, I know it is a somewhat feeble joke, but I have on occasion advocated that we could do worse than to erect a monument to Mrs Simpson who, however unintentionally, was of immense help to us Jews in removing an important pro-Hitler influence.

Racism

All this was a very long time ago, so let us now turn to matters of more recent concern. If, as I have already mentioned, there is, disregarding our greatly changed external circumstances, no particularly marked difference between our pre- and post-war positions, the obvious question is: how far have we actually progressed in being considered by the native population as 'one of them'. And, for that matter, how do we on our part deal with this question? Unsurprisingly, there is no clear-cut answer, if only because it depends to a considerable extent on individual circumstances. In particular, do we have children who are British-born or at any rate were quite small when they came to this country, or grandchildren, or other close British-born relatives? Have any of our children married a British-born citizen? In these cases we shall, in spite of any age gap, be automatically more involved than if we have no such direct link with the British-born generation. On another level, much depends on the work we do or did and our professional contacts at the time. But leaving this aside, I think we can identify quite a few relevant factors of more or less general validity for most of us refugees.

So, how far have we got? I believe the answer can be summed up for our generation of 'original refugees' with 'thus far and no further'. Before elaborating on this somewhat vague statement, allow me to be politically very incorrect: we show a good few distinguishing characteristics from the British-born, but colour is not one of them. Although I suppose there are some black Jewish refugees from Germany, personally I have never come across one. So, the question is whether the fact that we Jewish refugees are almost exclusively white has made life and integration any easier. Personally, I have no doubt that it did. Black people will find it more difficult to integrate than we did as long as the majority of the host population are white. Is this racist? It depends on how you define the term. I don't think I have to waste time belabouring the fact that as a Jew I don't regard any race different from mine as being inferior, let alone support the idea of persecuting it for any reason.

But matters are becoming far more complicated and controversial if it is a question of whether there are any grounds for holding the opinion that certain races have inborn characteristics that make them 'better' or 'worse' than others in particular areas. I have no really valid knowledge on this subject, but am convinced that not just a few but all races have and lack distinguishing talents and capabilities that make them in some ways better and in some ways less good than others. How could it possibly be otherwise? The fact that races often originate from different parts of the globe makes this already self-evident. Would you be surprised to learn that an Eskimo can stand the cold better than someone born in Havana, no matter where they happen to live? That Great Britain is a more naval country than Switzerland? Yet we have to be more than careful not to say something like this aloud the moment the question of colour enters the debate. I *am* presumably allowed to say that black people are better at some sports than whites. This does not make me a racist. But if I were to say that there are differences in intelligence between the races;

or, say, that white people are more capable mathematicians than black ones (and, of course, I have not the slightest idea whether this is true or whether the opposite is the case); or if I call members of another race, like the Duke of Edinburgh so memorably did, 'slitty-eyed' (which I happen to think can be very attractive in women); I would probably be accused of racism, provided that I compare unfavourably with my own a race whose members' skins are darker than mine.

I am afraid there appears to be no such sensitivity (in non-Jews) when it involves comments on the Jewish race, though it may be said that things are getting better in this area. The *Concise Oxford Dictionary* (4th edition) for instance, still contained the verb 'to jew' defining it as to cheat or overcharge; there is no trace of it in its 10th edition published in 1999. On the other hand, while 'Bah Bah Black sheep' or 'Ten little niggers' is now considered racially offensive and has to be 'cleansed', I have not heard of any request to clean up Dickens and make Fagin an Irishman, say, which ought to be easy without affecting the narrative at all. And it does not seem that the Commission for Racial Equality has had any sleepless nights about it. I wonder how it would react if someone were to raise the point, but I suspect I know. It remains an unfortunate fact that if you compare the Jewish race to any other, in nine out of ten cases it turns in some way into something derogatory – even if it is just damning with faint praise such as the statement that Jews are better at making money than most other races or look after their offspring better (not true). Or could we, as I have discussed in another chapter, be too sensitive about it? Perhaps, but more often than not we have good reason to be. (though I have not heard anybody of my race complaining about Dickens making Fagin a Jew, however unnecessarily).

I wonder, though, how we Jews would fare if we were to join in the game of protesting about 'political incorrectness'. I suspect that we would not get very far if we did. Coloured races are simply in a special category. Take the case of the late Professor Eysenck, who, on purely scientific grounds, tried to show that there were qualitative differences between the races, and was ferociously attacked for his pains, so much so that – or so I was told – he was considering changing his name in order to protect his children from any damage his findings might cause to them in their future lives. Again, I have no idea whether his findings were correct or not, but I am convinced of two things: firstly, that his conclusions had been arrived at entirely objectively. To attack him on anything other than scientific grounds was therefore utterly wrong. And secondly, if it had been the Jews who, in his opinion, were the inferior race, there would probably have been nothing like the same general outcry.

The foregoing remarks might be said to belong in this book's chapter on anti-Semitism. The reason why I have put them here is that I believe they do play a part in the way in which we refugees are regarded by the native population: a double whammy – of foreign origin *and* Jewish. It is a simple truth that the combination of these two factors make it more difficult for us to be fully 'accepted'.

However, do not let us judge others too harshly. For while most of us, and particularly former Jewish refugees, will strenuously deny being racist, and rarely are in the accepted sense, I am aware from personal experience that it is more likely than we think that we, too, can show quite unsuspected manifestations of it. Let me explain. A near relative of mine is married to a woman of mixed race. It genuinely never occurred to me to regard her as different in any way, except that, as it happens, she has forged a far more spectacularly successful professional career than her white husband. The marriage produced several daughters. Some of them, in their turn, married white, others black husbands. Not having kept in close touch with that branch of the family, I had lost track of which spouse is white and which is black. Who cares, anyway? It does not make the slightest difference. Until, some time ago, when I got into a lengthy correspondence with the father-in-law of one of those daughters. He was not personally known to me, but he was very interested in genealogy and anxious to learn all there was to know about my family tree. After having exchanged a number of letters on the subject, it occurred to me that, being relatives, it was not right that we should continue addressing each other as 'Mr' instead of by our first names. So I wrote and suggested the change and he readily agreed.

Some time later he sent me a photo of his family taken on the occasion of an anniversary celebration. He and some others were black! The point of the story? I got a jolt because I had suggested to a black man that we be on first name terms. Not that I regard myself in any way superior to him; for all I know he is a much better man than I am. Yet the fact that I found it in any way remarkable was a gut reaction of which I feel ashamed. It certainly runs contrary to all my genuinely-held convictions. So why should I have found this completely irrelevant difference in colour at all noteworthy? No good reason I can think of. But the fact is, I did. And hands up those who, if they are quite honest with themselves, are absolutely certain that they would have reacted differently! It taught me a surprising lesson about a fact whose existence I had been entirely ignorant of before: on some levels racial differences do play a part in our minds, whether we like it or not. Subconsciously we cannot overlook certain marked differences. If this is racist, so be it; in this form it is at least a comparatively harmless manifestation of the disease. But harking back to my original statement: is it surprising that black people will take (even) longer to integrate with a white population than we white Jewish immigrants with the British?

Once more – language!

As I have mentioned in my preface, our pronunciation, or rather the way in which we utter our words, even if correctly pronounced, has one certain effect: with very few exceptions, we shall always be recognised – even if not necessarily judged – for what we originally were: foreigners, ie not fully-fledged Englishmen or women. I maintain that almost anyone who has arrived in this country at an age older than 15 remains linguistically an 'alien' all his life, because he cannot hope to speak with a pure British accent. This even applies to actors obviously best qualified to adopt a correct pronunciation except, of course, those who trade on their foreign accent like some Frenchmen and Hungarians (Yes, I know Leslie Howard, a Hungarian by birth, had a perfect British accent, especially if you remember his film The Scarlet Pimpernel. But if he was older than 15 on arrival in this country, he must have been the exception that proves the rule.) And we refugees recognise our non-British brethren even better than the British do, being able quite often to distinguish between the English of, say, an ex-Berliner, a Bavarian or a Viennese. I remember my chagrin when one day I stopped my car at a red light, a driver next to me rolled down his window and asked, 'Could you please tell me the way to Bryanston Square?' 'Sorry,' I replied, and got no further. 'Na dann können wir ja auch Deutsch sprechen.' ('Well, in that case we might as well speak German.')

Such an incident may be regarded as representing something of a friendly recognition; but the British, whilst (hopefully) not holding it against us, have no such benevolent thoughts when they make no secret of the fact that they recognise us immediately as foreign-born. 'Where do you come from?' is the usual question. I am afraid an answer such as 'from Hampstead' is no good, being invariably followed by, 'No, I mean originally from what country?' I know of only one single case where a friend of mine, on being asked that question, replied, in order to cut matters short, 'Austria' and the questioner replied, 'No, I mean from which London district.' This incident was sufficiently rare, not to say sensational, to enable her to dine out on it, regularly causing amusement to her audience, provided it consisted of former refugees.

In spite of our obvious shortcomings in the pronunciation department, we sometimes speak and write a more correct English than the British person we happen to be conversing. But in most cases, our first language still comes to us more naturally. These days, the use of word processors makes it very easy to repeatedly change what we have written and in most cases to eventually arrive at, or at least approach the correct expression or construction of an English sentence. In fact you can overdo it. I myself know when to stop: the moment I realise that I am starting to change words or structures back to what I had considered incorrect before. Incidentally, this possibility of constant alteration is not generally approved by all the writing world. I once looked in, at a book fair, on a lecture given by a woman trying to recruit authors for Mills and Boon in whose publications good English is not necessarily the first requirement. She expressed the opinion that the word processor was the greatest enemy of writers, because it was apt to make authors linger too long on one sentence. Well, everybody is entitled to his or her opinion. But even with electronic help I still find it easier to write correct German than correct English, and this although I arrived in England as a young man and have spent more than two thirds of my life here. This is a generally known phenomenon: elderly German people who gradually lose their marbles forget English even if they have spent many decades in this country, and tend to revert to German. In these cases geriatricians recommend to younger relatives that they try to force their elders to speak English as much as possible so as to slow down the process of mental deterioration.

As a matter of fact, English is, for Germans, not a particularly difficult language to learn. But this has nothing to do with pronouncing it correctly. One other country, incidentally, where this phenomenon is even more marked is Holland, a country whose language is probably even easier for Germans to learn, but at the same time quite impossible to pronounce like a native. I started my emigration in Amsterdam, and Dutch friends of mine, when they wanted to have some fun, used to ask me to say 'Scheveningen', the name of a well-known Dutch spa near the Hague. As it happened, I spoke the language quite well (my mother was originally Dutch) but when I uttered that word, they invariably all burst out laughing, whereas I simply could not understand what was wrong with my pronunciation. I don't know whether this is true, but the story goes that, since Scheveningen is literally impossible for any non-Dutchman to pronounce correctly, the Dutch underground used to expose German spies in this simple way.

As regards the accent problem, interestingly, a British-born Jew with whom I once discussed the question remarked to me, 'Your accent is that of an English Jew', referring no doubt to second generation Polish and Russian Jews whose parents had arrived in this country late in the 19th and early in the 20th century and whose first language at home would probably have still been predominantly their native one. With most of them living in the East End of London, they probably heard initially 'pure' English comparatively rarely. Today, of course, that district has largely lost its undiluted Jewish character, with black immigrants tending to make it their first residence just as Jews did in former times.

Children of refugees

For most of us, one question required serious thought: whether or not to teach German at an early age to our children for whom it would be the second language. Usually they didn't hear much German at home. In my own family – and I am sure this was typical – we frequently did not even realise in which of the two languages we were conversing. Curiously enough, even some of those children who, on arrival in this country, were still small but old enough to have learnt German as their original language, are today no longer able to speak it properly; and many of those who do usually have a distinctly English accent – better than a German one when speaking English!

It is of course always an advantage to know as many languages as possible and, since German was our mother tongue, what was more logical than to see to it that our children should be better equipped than the average English person and learn it 'painlessly' from birth? This was the theory, but in practice it did not often work that way at all. There was, curiously enough, frequently a strong resistance on the part of the children. The exception were families in which grandparents shared the home; often they were too old or too set in their ways to learn English, so practically the only way of communication between them and the grandchildren was German. But those situations apart, it still seems surprising how comparatively few refugee children today speak German anything like fluently, if at all. One of the reasons is obvious: the war. During the period spanning from 1938 to, say, 1950, we adults strictly avoided speaking German in public, some of us even at home where it was not dangerous, so our children did not have much opportunity of hearing it. But even where this was not the reason, it seemed that many of the kids did not want to be different from their friends and classmates and apparently experienced some kind of reverse peer pressure strong enough for them to put up a passive resistance to learning our original language.

I used to wonder whether our children would, once

they had English friends, feel ashamed of their parents with their foreign accents and customs, and try to keep their mates away from us. I half expected it, but it did not happen, certainly not in my family, and as far as I know not with my acquaintances either; this, incidentally, in spite of the fact that children can often feel embarrassed by their parents' behaviour. I remember in my own childhood frequently being worried that when my parents came to my school or were in touch with my friends, they might commit a faux pas so horrible that it would make my position in the eyes of my peers impossible forever. Whilst this attitude does not seem to have changed, surprisingly it did not extend to any embarrassment about our foreign origins.

I felt it would be good for children of refugees to spend part of their developing years at a British boarding school, so as to give them the opportunity of a period of living in an 'undiluted' British atmosphere without any refugee influence. In fact my son became a boarder, my daughter did not. It is interesting to note that it did not make any marked difference to their development. Their daily attendance at school and the social intercourse with their native friends were quite sufficient to offset the atmosphere at home, provided their parents did nothing intentionally to keep Continental characteristics and customs alive. Today, owing to the fact that we have become such a multi-racial society, the problem has probably greatly diminished in practical importance. But at the time of which I speak, ie shortly after our arrival in Britain, we were one of the main 'multi' constituents in 'multi-racial'. These days you have only to look at a group of children in a primary school to realise that they mix perfectly well and give no thoughts whatever to racial differences. It makes you wonder at what age matters begin to change in so unfortunate a manner.

Another reason for children's resistance to being taught German, might have been simple inertia. Or could it be that refugee children simply do not want to speak the language of a country that had given their parents so much pain and has committed such unspeakable crimes against humanity? Sometimes this is put forward as the explanation. I wonder in fact whether it links up by any chance with the phenomenon on which I touched in a different chapter – namely that our grandchildren are often more interested in our antecedents and experiences than our children. But perhaps I am overdoing the psychological bit and there is a far more prosaic reason: the older ones among us have only to recall how we ourselves reacted to our parents' and uncles' stories about their experiences during the 1914-1918 War: the mass slaughter, the primitive state of medical science at the time and even the daily sight of a postman who might be carrying that dreaded War Office telegram are difficult to visualise today, even by those of us who lived through the period 1939-1945. But they must have been every bit as traumatic as our own experiences during the last war and under Hitler before emigration. But did we youngsters really want to know? By and large, the answer was no. Kids apparently just don't. They want to get on with their own lives.

It is no different with memories of the last war. 'War bores' are – however unjustifiably – the butt of many humorous stories. We have only to remember sitcoms such as Only Fools and Horses where Uncle Albert is being mercilessly ridiculed. Real Holocaust survivors, of course, are in a special category, but even here the situation is by no means an unambiguous one, as Anne Karpf, the daughter of the pianist Natalia Karpf, has graphically described in her book *The War After*.*

At any rate it points again to the somewhat unpalatable fact that stories and documentaries about the war and the Hitler times are often listened to or viewed with more attention by people who are not overly concerned personally, than by our nearest and dearest. As I pointed out elsewhere, for the former it has become 'history'.

Or am I in fact trying to see something that is not there? The reason might at least in part simply be that our children have heard the same stories over and over again, and/or can take them only in small doses. All in all it is an interesting question; I am afraid I do not have a really satisfactory answer to it.

Attitude to work

There can be no doubt that initially, when we observed the English at work, we felt that the frequently expressed opinion about the British as a nation being lazy when compared with the Germans was correct. The natives, on the other hand, felt that we worked far too hard and did not enjoy the really important things in life. Observing our often frantic efforts, they shook their heads and came out with the condescending old maxim 'The British work to live, the Germans live to work.' All well and good if you had been born here, but somewhat galling when you were a refugee endeavouring to get back to first base! The truth, of course, is far more complex.

The amount of work done by the members of a nation as a matter of course seems to a large extent to be the

---

* Published by William Heinemann in 1996 and Minerva Paperbacks in 1997.

result of culture and tradition. The wave of immigrants from countries like Kenya, India and Pakistan, which started some time after the flood of German Jewish refugees had exhausted itself, has shown this very clearly indeed. Newsagents and smaller supermarkets, open nearly if not all 24 hours of the day and night and often staffed by the proprietors themselves or members of their families, have clearly created a new and unique work ethic hitherto entirely unknown to Europeans. In normal circumstances no British, German, or any other national I can think of would wish to follow their example. The new trend for many British businesses to stay open for longer hours and on Sunday has nothing to do with this. It is made possible simply by shift work. Nor has it any connection with the financial need of those working so hard, at least not in the long run. After their defeat in World War II, the Germans certainly worked extremely hard and successfully, but with the completion of the *Wirtschaftswunder* (economic miracle) their enthusiasm for overtime distinctly waned. Many emigrants from Far Eastern countries, on the other hand, have become quite prosperous without showing any signs of wishing to change their working habits.

As a matter of fact, the reason why the British always had the reputation on the Continent, or at least in Germany, of taking life easier was almost certainly the British weekend. I remember, for instance, that a German midday paper many years ago found it worthwhile to print an illustrated article about it. But few people are likely to remember that at that time the 'weekend' merely meant British workers having the Saturday *afternoon* off. In Germany, this was by no means the absolute rule. And when I arrived in this country in 1934, Saturday *morning* work was still quite customary, although business firms had begun, as I gathered rather by way of concession, to limit attendance to a reduced – one could hardly have called it yet 'skeleton' – staff. Lloyd's, for instance, was still open for business. The five-day week, as a matter of right, came into being only after the last war.

Incidentally, I define 'work' in this context as paid work. Many of us observed with some amusement that an Englishman will insist on his unwritten right to knock off early on Friday afternoon ('Poet's day – Piss off early, tomorrow's Saturday') only to spend the weekend, uncomplainingly, in backbreaking labour in his garden or on some DIY job. Seen from this angle, I maintain that the British are in fact far more industrious than the Germans. It is only when it comes to getting money for what they do that their attitude becomes unique.

I remember a friend of mine telling me that he and his wife had been at an Italian or Spanish holiday resort, I forget which. We Northern Europeans usually believe that Southerners are lazy. But this is by no means generally true: my friend's wife saw, shortly before lunch on the last day of their stay, a piece of costume jewellery, a bracelet, by no means expensive, which she particularly liked, except for the colour of the stones. Did the shop also have it in red? 'No, but we can get it for you.'

'Sorry, we're leaving tomorrow morning.'

'That's all right,' – the expression 'no problem' had not yet been invented – 'we'll get it this afternoon and deliver it to your hotel.' Which they did. I believe it is true to say that if such a thing happened in this country, it would be regarded as the definitive exception proving the rule. This can be shown by the reaction of one of my friends' acquaintances, to whom, greatly impressed, they related this experience as an example of some foreign countries' efficiency and willingness to give good service. The unexpected reaction from their listener was the comment, 'How very sad! Just think how badly these people must need the money if they are prepared to work that hard!'

I myself once had a basically similar experience. As an insurance broker, I did a good deal of business with foreign correspondents. One day we received a rather complicated and difficult enquiry. However, from a recent similar case I was immediately able to pinpoint the market where I could place this business on favourable terms and obtained a suitable quotation within an hour. When I told the head of the appropriate department to send a telex to the client forthwith (fax, let alone e-mail, was still a thing of the distant future) I got the, to me, astounding reply: 'No, let them wait for two days, otherwise they'll think it's too easy.' The idea that there can be pride and satisfaction in work well done and service given quickly did not occur to either of these two people. I do not have sufficient experience to be able to say whether it is general, but if so, I feel that this is one British attitude which it is undesirable to assimilate.

But let us not be too harsh. It is not impossible for the same to happen in countries with an established reputation for good service, which is sometimes more apparent than real. I remember on a business trip to the US (where my partner was running an associate company) trying to make an appointment with a firm of brokers I wanted to interest in a type of insurance my London outfit happened to specialise in. I explained the nature of the proposition to an employee in the New York broking firm. 'Sorry,' the man replied, 'our vice president' – in the US it is always a vice president – 'is abroad and won't be back until late on Thursday.' This was Tuesday and I was going back the following Saturday. 'But I'm sure our vice president will be very interested. I'll phone him and arrange for you to see him on Friday. I'll let you know.'

'Terrific,' I said to my partner as we left, 'in London they would no doubt have said something like: "You won't be able to see him earlier than next week. Sorry this will be too late for you, but it can't be helped." ' The only trouble was that during the rest of my stay I never heard from that firm again until a Lloyd's underwriter told me some months later that he had received a direct approach from them with regard to the same type of insurance I had mentioned to them. You can't always make generalisations on isolated cases of attitudes and behaviour.

Refugee Organisations

These played a very important role for refugees both in a general and charitable way during the early days and in many cases they still do. Their value has been so fully acknowledged and documented in many publications that I will do no more than touch upon a few points. Firstly, their future. Clearly, it is inescapable that with the gradual disappearance of the original refugee generation and that which immediaely followed, the importance of these undertakings is bound to diminish progressively. Our next-but-one generation cannot, by any stretch of imagination, be called 'refugees' or even former refugees. This is a progression as natural as it is welcome – the third generation are no longer 'aliens'. The organisations and the numerous officers and executives who have often served them for so long and devotedly deserve our highest gratitude and praise. But the usefulness of most of their work is bound to come to an end at some time.

There exists, however, an interesting phenomenon: many of the people running them do not want to acknowledge this. They shut their eyes and ears to it and make strenuous efforts to keep members of the next but one generation as involved as ours was. But the fact has to be faced that, whatever their historical importance, most of our offspring simply aren't interested in them. The people actively concerned may find this disappointing, but should they really? New generations have their own problems which require their full attention and they simply do not have the time, energy and, let's face it, inclination to allow organisations whose importance is increasingly becoming a thing of the past to play more than a tangential part in their lives. The Huguenots were certainly an important emigration movement, and being a descendant of a Huguenot family may still be regarded as noteworthy. But, though I confess I have no detailed knowledge, I venture to doubt that there are many societies of former Huguenots in existence or regarded as necessary. They belong to the distant past and as such have their important, interesting, but no longer topical place in history.

Anxious though they may be to perpetuate themselves, the attitude of today's refugee organisations towards their older members is sometimes ambivalent. It is fully understandable that in the interest of efficient functioning there has to be an age limit for active officers. But I have always considered it a mistake to cast the original members lightly aside. They represent the last living links with the past which it is in the interest of these societies to preserve; as such they should be treated accordingly in positions where they can do no harm but their knowledge, personal experience and sometimes prestige can be preserved and utilised. By weeding them out, the organisers proceed in exactly the opposite direction from the one they mean to go.

Personally, as the reader will have realised, I see no great merit in making undue efforts to preserve something which, through the passage of time, is gradually losing its *raison d'être*. But I also appreciate that a reduction in the activities of such an organisation can cause unexpected difficulties in practice. The German-Jewish Old Age Homes offer a good illustration. Originally there were long waiting lists for them. For obvious reasons these became shorter and shorter until by now they have virtually disappeared. As a result, some of the Homes have become surplus to requirements and have been closed and/or the whole organisation has been amalgamated with an English-Jewish charitable organisation. However, in spite of the decline in numbers of the 'original' Jewish immigrants, we have to anticipate that there will be an (albeit ever-decreasing) demand for places in refugee old age homes for the next 20 years. The obvious consequence must be that old refugees, becoming as they are an ever-smaller minority, will find themselves in homes run on English-Jewish lines. In theory there should be no difference. But as I describe elsewhere, the tendency on the part of the older generation is demonstrably still to keep to its own original fellow countrymen and women, notwithstanding the fact that Jewish immigration from Germany into this country started over 65 years ago and that a considerable degree of assimilation has inevitably taken place. This is obviously not a question of race as such, but has to do with the different culture, history, upbringing, tradition, surroundings and, last but not least, basic attitudes that divide English and German Jews, except possibly the very orthodox ones.

I have quite frequently experienced Jewish refugees becoming irritable in English-Jewish company and regarding it as discourteous that the latter keep on discussing the activities of friends, acquaintances and associations that the former have never heard of. Of course, the opposite might also be the case, but in any event the result could well be that the two kinds are far less likely to mix happily than one would hope. With refugees in the minority in Jewish homes, I can foresee a certain amount of unhappiness which it will take a great deal of tact and diplomacy to overcome, as I hope and trust will happen. This, I need hardly add, is in no way a value judgement, but simply a recognition of certain differences in the character and attitudes of the two strands of Jewry, not least as regards the question of tolerance.

I experienced an instructive illustration of the latter at a time when, demand for places in old age homes still vastly exceeded supply. I was a member of the Jewish Refugee Homes Management Committee, which consisted of former German Refugees and English Jews, the latter being in a slight majority. One day we received an application for admission from an old German gentile couple. There was ample and wholly convincing evidence that during the Nazi period they had conducted themselves in an exemplary fashion, helping German Jews wherever they could, so much so that the husband had for some time been in a concentration camp on account of his attitude and activities. We all knew, of course, how very dangerous life had been in Germany for open sympathisers with Jews. To some extent they had been unsung heroes. To me and my fellow refugees, any 'Aryan' who could actually prove his or her extraordinary courage and idealism in these matters commanded the greatest respect and admiration. For while there was no occasion for German Jews to be particularly brave – resistance was absolutely useless; anything we did or had done could not prevent our being regarded as vermin and being treated as such – gentile Germans who associated themselves with us by word or deed did so entirely beyond the call of duty. Thus, if there was any way in which I, as a member of Self Aid (about which more anon) or the Homes Management Committee could be useful to them, I was only too anxious to do it.

This attitude was fully shared by my German-Jewish colleagues on the committee, and we readily voted for the gentile couple to be admitted as residents of one of the Homes as soon as possible. Not so, however, the British committee members. As a body, they voted against the proposal. The homes were a Jewish charity, intended for the benefit of Jews as the Trust Deed clearly stated, and admitting any non-Jew for whatever reason was simply not on. Our representations that here was a special and exceedingly meritorious case fell on deaf ears. Our English colleagues, dedicated though they were to the good cause, just did not understand. Hence, the applicants had to be advised that their request had been refused. According to the letter of the law the refusal was justified, but there would have been no harm whatever in making an exception. I seriously considered resigning from the committee and I am still a little surprised that I didn't. I shudder to think what the two old people must have felt about the gratitude of the Jewish race. With hindsight, I am bound to add that we were probably doing them a favour. I very much doubt that in the long run they would really have fitted into the culturally so different environment of a Jewish Home. But this, of course, was not the point.

The episode, small in itself, does show up one of the general differences between English and originally German Jewish cultures. In my opinion, it cannot be explained on religious grounds – it has different roots. I think it has something to do with what I call the 'non-integration tendency' of British Jewry. I cannot repeat often enough that this is not to deny in any way the enormous amount of Jewish charitable work that was being done in the 1930s and was of the greatest help to many of us; though it is worth acknowledging that Jewish charities were by no means the only ones: organisations, for example those run by Quakers, did an outstanding amount of good as well. But somehow or other one often felt, rightly or wrongly, that the reason for the former was not so much compassion for us – our tendency to integrate was in some circles and against all the evidence still regarded as wholly misguided and one of the causes of our misfortune – but the simple and natural wish of Jews to help other Jews, whatever their merits.

Clearly, Jewish refugees themselves were not normally in a position to be charitable, but there were exceptions. Among them was the 'Self Aid of Refugees' I have already briefly mentioned, an organisation that had originally been created through the generosity of a number of better-off Hitler refugees. In spite of its small size it did very useful and necessary work. Its funds, apart from the (for them at the time) substantial sums provided by its founders, stemmed from small voluntary contributions by the refugee community and an annual concert, which for many years it fell to me to organise. When we needed a prominent patron, the Countess of Harewood, herself the daughter of refugees of mixed race and a gifted pianist to boot, inevitably sprang to mind. But how to approach her correctly? My experience did not extend to social contacts with Earls and their wives. But I had a slight acquaintance with her father, a very distinguished musicologist and for me the archetype of an absentminded professor. So I rang him up: 'Please forgive my troubling you, but how do I address your daughter?' Long pause for thought, then: 'I don't really know, I always call her Marion.' I eventually got the necessary information from somewhere else and for many years she very kindly presided as patron of the concerts.

In later years, Self Aid derived a considerable proportion of its funds from the international Heirless Jewish Property Fund, painstakingly and skilfully collected by an organisation especially formed for this task. It traced Jewish assets originally confiscated by the Germans whose previous owners could, due to the Holocaust, no longer be identified. A large number of Jewish charitable organisations all over the world profited and could provide financial help which would otherwise have been entirely beyond their horizons. By that time I had become Self Aid chairman and in this capacity attended the half-yearly meetings designed to allocate money to the various British charitable organisations. The meetings were something of an anomaly, the participants on the one hand being applicants for funds and on the other decision makers about the allocations for others, a dual role which was a somewhat hilarious contradiction in itself. No wonder that most of the decisions were made by the very forceful chairman of the committee and usually agreed by those present with a minimum of discussion. It is interesting to recall that one exception was the Wiener Library, always extremely hard-up during its initial struggle for survival and therefore a regular applicant. Considering the outstanding importance of this institution today, it is, with hindsight, surprising that so many voices were raised trying to deny it the full support it needed and deserved. It is to the lasting credit of the committee's chairman that he always used his authority in its favour.

Without having to fear an accusation of undue modesty, I may say that my contribution as Self Aid chairman may be regarded as largely undistinguished. But it did give me some valuable insights into the interplay between charitable work and human nature. In this respect, I doubt that there are particularly marked differences between the attitudes of diverse nationalities and cultures. There can, of course, be no question that it is very praiseworthy indeed for individuals to devote time and effort to charitable work. Yet, there is another side to the coin. This is not the place to go fully into the motivations of the average part-time charitable worker, but I am afraid I have been forced to the reluctant conclusion that in certain respects it can be bad for – or at least, can show up weaknesses in – the characters of the active participants. I am referring not to the collection but to the distribution end of charitable funds.

The Self Aid committee, which met once a month to decide on or confirm charitable awards, consisted of a number of dedicated and praiseworthy people of both sexes. It based its decisions, of course, on need. So far so good. But not infrequently a second factor raised its ugly head: that of the 'deserving case'. Nobody except a judge in a criminal court ought to be allowed to make value judgements on this basis. To the average citizen it can give an entirely unwarranted and undeserved authority which can have unfortunate results not only for his or her character – no great harm done – but more so for those considered, to quote Bernard Shaw, the undeserving poor who may not be assisted to the degree they ought to be. The question of when a case was 'undeserving' in spite of the undoubted need, was more than tricky.

There were, for instance, one or two people among our 'clients' who were very orthodox Jews, and produced annual offspring with mind-numbing regularity. Naturally, they were never out of financial straits. Well, they were the authors of their own misfortune, with religious and physical satisfaction in addition. Was there really a case for encouraging them? Others could find no work, or so they said: laziness, too choosy, inadequate or genuine? On the lighter side I remember the case of a lonely elderly woman who got into debt because, as it turned out, she had overspent trying to keep a boyfriend younger than herself. (You should have heard the views of the female committee members about that one! How I managed to persuade them to help this lady I still don't know, but I did it). One of the most striking cases I can remember was that of a man whose wife had had to undergo a life-saving cancer operation. He had no money but had managed, God knows how, to borrow a sufficient sum to obtain the services of one of the foremost cancer surgeons. He had known that he would never be able to repay the debt and came to us for assistance. 'No way,' some committee members said, 'he had no right to do what he did and deserves no help.' Until I pointed out that, while what he had done had been quite wrong, if I had been in the same position – no money and a desperately ill wife – I only hoped that I would have had the guts to act in the same way this man had done. Interestingly enough, here too the female members of the committee were against, the males were for this man. He got the money. I can't decide who was right, but it goes to show the heavy responsibility of charity workers ill equipped and subject to the same prejudices we all are, when making decisions about morality often leading to unfortunate practical results.

Something else struck me. There can be no question that the main purpose of any charitable institution should be to work itself out of existence, ie become unnecessary as soon as possible. I know that this is a pipe dream that can be achieved only very rarely indeed. There is too much poverty, persecution and misery in this world. But the guiding principle remains – the less necessary a charitable institution becomes, the more successful it is. But to my surprise I found that charitable workers on the one hand naturally and selflessly make every effort to fulfil the purpose for which their organisation has been founded; but that they, on the other hand, usually are most reluctant to 'let go' in the sense that they would feel deprived if their work suddenly turned out to have become unnecessary. I even observed instances where they turned against the possibility of carrying out their work with greater efficiency. I had come to the conclusion early-on that there would be many advantages in amalgamating Self Aid with the main refugee association, the AJR. This would have affected neither its purpose nor its working methods, but it would have helped to reduce the cost of its general administration and thereby leave more money for the purpose it had been created for. But my proposal to this effect was strongly resisted, although most of the dissenters were themselves AJR members. 'We don't want anything to do with *them*!' Clearly, everybody was anxious to keep his own little empire intact – for his or her own satisfaction; there certainly was no financial gain in it. Charitable work, while necessary, desirable and commendable, has sometimes, like most of our actions, subconscious motivations that go beyond the entirely altruistic.

The work was not without its slightly hilarious incidents. At that time, several frauds committed by charitable officers came to public attention: honorary officials had diverted some of the contributions into their own pockets. There was not the slightest reason to suppose that this would ever happen in Self Aid – for one thing its assets were far too small to be attractive – but at the same time it was clear that those organisations where it *had* happened had been equally convinced of the absolute integrity of those who turned out to be the culprits. Being an insurance broker I felt that, if by any chance anything like this should occur in an organisation presided over by me, I would become a general laughing stock. I therefore decided to take out insurance against embezzlement. As is well-known, an insurance like this is always a very delicate matter: those people against whose possible misdemeanours you want to insure, ie those who, by handling and having responsibility for the money, represent the real risk, if any, are normally the most respected members of the organisation in question. Therefore most of them would regard it as deeply offensive that you were taking out insurance against them committing a fraudulent act.

There is only one way out; you have to insure the whole lot, without exception, from office junior to honorary chairman. This is what I did. It so happened that the honorary president and founder member of Self Aid (who of course took no active part in its running) was Sir Sigmund Warburg, the well-known banker whose clients had entrusted him with looking after assets worth hundreds of millions. He automatically became one of those whose dishonesty I covered against. It never ceased to amuse me that I had insured a man like him against embezzlement, not only because of who and what he was but also because the amounts 'at risk' were probably less than his company's petty cash account. Of course, I never told him; he was a somewhat prickly gentleman who would almost certainly not have appreciated the humour of the situation and have resigned forthwith.

Nationality

But back to more typical refugee experiences. I have already discussed the 'Where do you come from syndrome'. Equally painful is the question 'What is your nationality?' Being naturalised, the correct answer is, of course, 'British', but, again, this is not what the questioner has in mind. He wants to know what country we belonged to originally. This, to me, is a sure sign that the British, however liberal and tolerant they may be (or think they are), do not regard someone naturalised as 'really' British. This does not, of course, extend to members of the next generation, who are, after all, British-born and therefore not dependent on their parents' naturalisation. But vis-à-vis us, the immigrants, it is a gut reaction though without malice.

I had a good illustration of this on one occasion in my own business. I had succeeded in arranging some fairly specialised, though not unique, insurance for a large state-run organisation. One might have expected such an organisation to do business by preference with British professional firms if available, as was the case here. Obviously, therefore, they regarded me as British. So I was greatly taken aback when the head of its insurance department, with whom I was dealing and was on the friendliest personal terms, on one occasion let slip a remark that made it quite clear he still regarded me as a foreigner after all, even though it had not affected his professional judgement – a sure sign that he had not intended to be offensive. There can be no doubt that all this must have its effect on our own estimate of the position we occupy in British society.

'Thank you Britain Fund'

Let's face it, many of us are in some respects still ambivalent in our feelings towards Great Britain. When we came here, we were very thankful indeed to find refuge. And there can be little doubt that British Jewry played a large, never to be forgotten part in this acceptance and the means for it. Yet with a more liberal attitude on the part of the British authorities as a whole, a great many more German Jews could almost certainly have been saved. I will not conceal the feeling of bitterness I experienced when, on the occasion of the Russian invasion of Hungary after the last war, the British

Government decided on the spot to accept any Hungarian refugee who wanted to come to this country with no questions asked. Remembering the unspeakable treatment meted out to Hungarian Jews during the Nazi period and how many ex-Nazis, not to say war criminals, must have been among the anti-Communists being given asylum without any examination of their antecedents, one was bound to ask oneself – why could *we* not have been received as freely at the time of our deadly peril? Especially when we consider that German Hitler Refugees cost the British authorities very little money, gave next to no trouble and played their full part wherever and whenever they could. On balance there can really be no doubt that, in addition to the really prominent men and women of art and science whom Britain was only too glad to welcome, we, the ordinary citizens, have proved to be of considerable value as well.

No wonder then that there was (and to some extent still continues to be) some discussion and controversy when the plan of the Thank You Britain Fund was mooted. The idea was, of course, to thank this country for having received us in our hour of need, and to express this by an annual Thank You Britain Fund lecture given by a British citizen highly prominent in his field. In spite of the reservations I have just expressed, I believe that on balance the Fund idea was right. Yes, more could have been done. Yes, we amply repaid the hospitality we received. At the same time, the amount of goodwill shown to most of those lucky enough to reach these shores was considerable and no doubt saved many lives. So it was only right and proper that we should thank our then hosts for what we received even if some of us think it could have been more.

I hope I have been able to convey a flavour of what it meant to be a Jewish refugee immigrant into Britain. The answer to the question how far we have actually got and whether there can be any further development is the subject of the final chapter.

So, what next?

I

When one of my children got married, we gave a reception to which, of course, not only our children's but also our own friends were invited. Looking through the completed list of our own guests, I exclaimed with astonishment: 'Where are the British?' For indeed, there were next to no English (as opposed to anglicised) names to be seen. And this despite me having spent more than half my life in Great Britain. I was running a business in which all my co-directors were British-born; I had plenty of non-refugee clients; my business contacts, the insurers, many of whom I was on friendly terms with, were largely British; and I was a member of Lloyd's – a British Institution if ever there was one, whatever you may think of it. Then why were practically none of my 'genuinely' British contacts included in the list of invitees? A good question. To answer it, I shall have to start by dealing with matters which at first glance may not seem to have much to do with our original theme. But if you will bear with me I hope that the connection will become apparent as we go along.

In a previous chapter I have already answered with 'Thus far and no further' the question of how far we refugees had got in establishing ourselves in the eyes of British-born people as 'true Englishmen'. But why have we got 'no further'? Is it simply our inability – possibly because of our indelible foreign accents – to adapt still more, however much we genuinely wish to, or are there other reasons? I strongly believe the latter.

What do we German-Jewish refugees actually represent in British society? A 'group'? This would mean more cohesion than in fact exists. An 'ethnic minority'? Clearly not. A 'category? Doesn't sound right. A 'class'? Unlikely, as we already belong to one of the usual classes, and it is difficult to visualise somebody belonging to more than one. (Difficult, but not impossible. Look at football stars, leading Labour politicians and so on: they belong, at least for some time, to special elite classes, but equally in many cases still to the working class. But this hardly applies to refugees.)

Anyway, nothing seems to fit exactly. Nevertheless, let us look at *The Concise Oxford Dictionary*'s definition of 'class' as it concerns us here: 'A system that divides members of a society into sets based on perceived social or economic status.' While we are about it, what about 'class consciousness': 'Awareness of one's status in a system of social class.' These two sound more likely to have some application to refugees, especially if we think of the words 'perceived' and 'awareness' applying not only to the attitudes of refugees but equally those of their British hosts. Thus, though refugees can hardly be regarded as a class as such, there are sufficient similarities for us to look at the question from this angle.

But halt! Aren't we always told that by now we are in the happy position of being a classless society? Well, according to an NOP in the year 2000, 85 per cent of Britons still think of Britain as class-based with almost as many believing that top jobs are only given to the privileged few. Almost 50 per cent consider themselves 'working class', a large percentage 'middle class', 18 per cent 'upper middle class' and 1 per cent 'upper class'. This is hardly the classless society in which, according to our politicians, we are living. One of the mistakes they and many other people make is to equate class almost entirely with material wealth, disregarding, to a large extent, culture, learning, the arts etc.

It is true, of course, that our society often goes to great lengths to try and create equal opportunities for all. But the aim here is much less to enable the population to acquire and enjoy more 'culture', than to give more of them a chance of finding better, ie better-paid, occupations. This is not to belittle in any way the work of local councils and a great many institutions offering further adult education. They are doing a splendid job, but in the majority of courses offered the same idea is uppermost: to 'better oneself' by acquiring more knowledge and thereby more chances of material advancement. This is not by any means true in every case; there are many quite excellent courses in art, music, history etc. But I cannot offhand recall any political party programme containing the promise to create places of learning specifically designed for the better appreciation of Rembrandt or Beethoven, and I doubt that if any party were to incorporate this in its propaganda, there would be much spin in it. It is the question of material circumstances that is foremost in both the government's and the bulk of the citizens' minds. Cultural factors and social standing are secondary.

But not necessarily as far as refugees are concerned. They all belong, of course, by now, to different classes with differing material wealth. Yet they are 'perceived' not through the prism of wealth, but through a non-material one – their immigrant status. Their children, on the other hand, whilst obviously not shedding their connection with their refugee parents, are almost invariably no longer regarded as refugees, a clear indication that the difference is social, cultural and, if you like, historic.

II

Whether you are a refugee or not, getting on in life, ie becoming qualified for a better position will mean in many instances moving up into a higher class. This can have its difficulties, but it is a positive step. However, what is the position of a person moving into a lower class? Here I can fall back on my own experience as well as that of many other refugees. Initially, most of us had to be content with jobs and activities vastly inferior to those to which we had been accustomed or trained for. Such a situation offers no particular hardship if you know or have at least every hope that it will be for a limited period only. In that case you do not change class. Generally, when we are young, we will readily accept a position as a lowly trainee, or an obligatory period of work that brings us into contact with the 'lower classes', because we know that this is necessary if we are to achieve higher things and that we have not lost membership of our own class. Similarly, for many not particularly military-minded persons, National Service was bearable mainly because they knew it was nothing but an interruption of their career and status for a limited period.

But it is a very different picture if we are stuck in an occupation which demands nothing near the qualifications we possess. If there is no reasonable expectation of being able to get out of it in the foreseeable future, if ever, we really have moved into a class lower than the one we originally occupied. This is not only bound to cause great unhappiness and frustration, but will also make it very unlikely that we will give of our best. Some refugees were initially in that position and it is to their credit that so many overcame it.

Am I exaggerating? I don't think so, for I had confirmation of my views in my own insurance broking business in quite a different context. For some time after the last world war, there was an acute shortage of trained staff. I therefore had the idea of employing university graduates (who at that time, as today, frequently had great difficulty finding a job in keeping with their qualifications) and training them in our profession. Surely people of their calibre would find it easy to learn what was, after all, an interesting occupation and would thereby become very useful members of the commercial community. A firm specialising in placing graduates in employment supplied us with a list of candidates and we successively employed no fewer than four of them. They were all utter failures. They clearly felt that the job opportunities offered them were in no way commensurate with what they expected from life; hence they were unhappy, frustrated and, whether they realised it or not, reluctant to make any real effort. I could understand their feelings. During the war I had been employed in a factory as an unskilled labourer – a very unskilled one. My wife subsequently always maintained that her main war effort had been to stop me from committing suicide due to a deep depression caused by the mind-numbing war work I was doing without any hope of advancement.

From facts like these it is clear that dropping into a lower class than one's original one can be very painful. I am, however, not trying to sing the praises of refugees who coped with it, but would like, if I may, to digress for a moment, to make another point that has always puzzled me. The main aim of any government's educational programme is to help people advance rather than let them remain static or even descend into a lower class – a misfortune that ought to happen to as few people as possible. However, considering the disparity in numbers between qualified and unqualified occupations (however necessary and important the latter undoubtedly are) is it wise to train up considerably more people for higher occupations than will probably eventually be needed? Is it desirable to do so without having made reasonably sure that there will be sufficient positions to fill? I have no knowledge of Government thinking on this, but can we be certain that the authorities, in their efforts to propagate and provide 'Higher Education', have made reliable estimates regarding the job prospects of those thus qualified? I rather doubt it or else we would not hear so much of graduates unable to find positions commensurate with their training and in consequence having to eventually be satisfied with occupying – at least as far as their jobs are concerned – a lower class than that for which their qualifications had originally prepared them.

III

Being unhappy if we move into a lower class should conversely mean greater happiness when moving in the opposite direction. And in many instances this is the case. But to what extent? If we look at the question of how many people really strive to move up into a higher class than their original one, we may be in for a surprise: I hope to show that while many people are anxious to achieve higher status, most of us do not really wish to leave our class once we have become established in it (whether this happens to be high or low) and move upwards. Or, to put it another way, the majority of us, once we have reached maturity, feel most comfortable in the class into which we have been placed and would feel out of our depth in others. Most of us, therefore, not only make little effort to leave our original class but, if it comes to the crunch, may make positive albeit subconscious efforts to stay in it.

It is not a good idea to try to prove a theory on the basis of anecdotal evidence, but allow me to start with it, because it will best explain what I have in mind. When I was doing war work, I remember one day getting a splinter under my nail, a very insignificant but nevertheless painful injury. 'Let me have a look,' said one of my colleagues, a very bright chap, older than me. I became apprehensive when he produced an exceedingly dirty and rusty pocket knife. But he proceeded to dig out the offending object extraordinarily skilfully and without giving me the slightest pain or discomfort. I was impressed. 'You should have become a surgeon!' I exclaimed.

'Well, in fact, I thought about it, but then decided not to bother,' he replied. One should not assess surgical skill on the basis of one removed splinter, but at the time his answer surprised me. Didn't we all strive to get on to higher things? Obviously only to a limited extent, within our orbit, as it were. So, my friend would no doubt have been quite pleased to become a foreman, but he did not want to become a surgeon. He was perfectly satisfied to remain in the class into which he had been placed by birth and upbringing

Was he an exception? In a manner of speaking, yes: many children do train for and move into a higher class than the one they were born into. But for an adult I very much doubt it. Speaking for myself, I am perfectly content to stay where I am. I have no urgent wish (though I wouldn't mind!) to be super-rich, certainly none to see my name in *Hello*, and I would feel entirely out of my depth with the 'landed gentry'. Equally I have no wish to become working class. During war work I got on excellently with my mates but, without being in the least snobbish, I always remained conscious of a cultural gap based, no doubt, on our different upbringings. And so, I am sure, did my colleagues. But neither of us had any wish for things to change. I remember that it was customary during the war for factories to broadcast on their internal loudspeakers 'Music while you work'. One day they played a frightfully jazzed-up version of Tchaikovsky's First Piano Concerto. Hackneyed though this piece is, this 'improvement' made my hair stand on end. 'You have no idea how much better this sounds in the original,' I remarked. 'Oooh, classical ...' was the only reply I got. They were satisfied with what they heard and did not want anything different. Indeed they felt that classical music was 'out of their class' (an erroneous opinion which the music industry has done as yet too little to try to correct).

The very few examples I have given are not, of course, sufficient proof in themselves that my opinion is correct. But I believe that if we accept it, we can find explanations for our own attitude towards our immigrant status. How genuine is our wish to become fully-fledged Englishmen? Could there be any subconscious tendencies working against it? Ours might not even be the only instance. Look, for example, at the ascent to sudden fame and riches of the successful super-sportsmen, pop artists, TV personalities and such, quite a few of whom come from humble beginnings. We hear every so often that they wasted the millions they earned in the most ridiculous manner, buying several homes, expensive cars, gambling, drinking, taking drugs, throwing parties costing hundreds of thousands a time, going through several super-expensive weddings and subsequent divorces etc – and ending up penniless in middle or old age. 'Ah, they just couldn't handle their sudden wealth,' I hear you say. This is no doubt true – but the question is, why couldn't they? All they had to do was not throw their money about. There is no reason why they should be less level-headed than others. In any case, members of the working classes are very often, through sheer necessity, past masters at managing what they earn. Why should this quality suddenly be lost? And in any event, those who acquire sudden wealth are certainly not going to lack offers of good advice on how to preserve it. But many of them still squander it in the most amazing manner, compulsively and deliberately. If we equate this with the subconscious desire to return to their original status, it is not enough to laugh this explanation off as ridiculous. Hands up those who can offer a better one.

Members of the working or middle classes who move up and are satisfied to do so are usually either great writers, thinkers or artists who may be said to be 'between classes' anyway. Or they are businessmen or women who, through their own efforts, enterprise, originality, hard work – and luck! – have become very successful and wealthy. They are obviously of a calibre that does not give them any reason to wish to return to a lower level. But here another phenomenon rears its ugly head: not a few of them (the Maxwells, the Tiny Rowlands and the Al Fayeds of this world) are, or were, in spite of the position they have achieved, not accepted by the Establishment, defined by *The Concise Oxford Dictionary* as 'a group in society exercising power and influence over matters of policy, opinion or taste, and seen as resenting change.' I shall have more to say about this shortly.

IV

As we have seen, the definition of class does to some extent apply to us, the original Hitler refugees. In our case it makes no difference that it is confined almost exclusively to only one generation. (The same may not necessarily be the case with the wave of refugees which originated towards the end of the 20th century, because assimilation in their case may, for a variety of reasons, be at a much slower pace; but that is another story.) We have also seen that with members of a particular class, conscious and unconscious desires about advancing from it can be in contradiction. Taking our own case, we continue to harbour a constant conscious desire to become more and more 'English' and to be accepted by the natives as such. What, if any, indications are there that this may be to a greater or lesser extent contrary to our subconscious wishes? I believe there are several.

There is first of all the fact that we are members of a minority. Such people not only tend to stick together (if only to better defend themselves against the genuine or perceived hostility of the majority), they also feel most comfortable with each other. In addition, they can usually easily recognise one another as of the same origin and find some pleasure in doing so, irrespective, incidentally, of whether they happen to be German, Austrian, Czechoslovakian, Polish or whatever. One might think that it is our common Jewishness that triggers off this recognition. Not so. I have already mentioned elsewhere the episode of sitting in a German restaurant and, forgetting where I was, classing every German entering – among whom there can hardly have been any Jews at all – as 'one of ours'. It does show that it is not only the accent, but also the general demeanour, so different from that of the British in many imperceptible ways, that is the key.

Secondly, the relative lengths of the periods spent in the two countries is of far less significance than where we spent our formative years. This is also important linguistically. As I have already mentioned, I myself can still instinctively recognise the incorrect construction of a German sentence much more easily – as my editor will be only too willing to confirm – than that of an English one, although I have spent almost three quarters of my life in England (but not the all-important first one).

A third reason is the attitude of the British themselves. It cannot by any means be called 'hostile', but there is a great difference between hostility and non-acceptance. It is not the British way to let us forget that we are not 'one of them'. And it affects us. In this respect all British citizens that we encounter represent the Establishment. Remember the definition? 'A group in society exercising ... influence over matters of policy, opinion or taste and seen to be resisting change.' Let us forget 'policy', where there are frequently no differences – many ex-refugees are staunchly Conservative, Liberal or Labour. It is the 'opinions and tastes' that are frequently different. The British Establishment resists our joining them because they have no desire to let people in who might mean change. To them, without their knowing it, we represent such change. We are like foreign organs which, as we all know, are rejected if surgically implanted into a person's body. The rejection does not only occur unintentionally but is, in medical cases, clearly against the recipient's conscious wishes and interests. But it is there. In medicine we make the greatest efforts to suppress and overcome this bodily resistance, but, unsurprisingly, there exists no parallel regarding the British attitude towards us 'foreign bodies'. This is not by any means an accusation, but it is apt to affect our own attitude in turn.

In the circumstances I believe that the lack of real social intercourse with the natives is in at least equal part of the hosts', not the foreigners' making. This is by no means only a British characteristic, but to my knowledge applies to many other countries as well. I had a friend, a very interesting, charming and gregarious man who was in a prominent and influential professional position. He had been living in France for many years. He once told me that he could count the number of really good French friends on fewer than the fingers of one hand. And another, who had gone to live in Switzerland as a tax haven, almost decided to leave again when, after trying for a few years, he had found it impossible to get on really good social terms with a single Swiss family (however, financial considerations prevailed). It seems to be different in the USA, where in some parts of the country, a considerable proportion of the population, insofar as their forbears did not arrive on the 'Mayflower', consist of later immigrants themselves. And as regards Australia, I had an acquaintance who had been interned in that county during the war and subsequently decided to settle there. He told me, only half-jokingly, that in his new home country there was little discrimination: more often than not the 'old families' had been founded by the black sheep of English families who had been more or less emphatically made to emigrate to Australia where, surprisingly, they had made good beyond anybody's expectations.

The British, whose attitude is certainly not designed to make us 'comfortable', are bound to produce in us a certain amount of ambivalence, a mixture of wishing to be accepted and hostility because we know we aren't. As a result, we do stick to the group where we can let ourselves go, be ourselves, have common memories, traditions and culture and don't have to be on our guard in case we commit a faux pas which, in the eyes of others, is letting us down. It is so much easier for like to stick to like.

Of course, there are exceptions, most of which I have already mentioned earlier in this book: the passport Englishmen; the deliberate total assimilators resolutely cutting themselves off from their co-refugees; and the artists and academics whose entry into this country was deliberately promoted by the British community and who were accepted not in spite of but because of their foreign status. Their peculiarities as foreigners are not only overlooked but possibly an admired asset. In other words, they feel comfortable in British circles because they are made comfortable.

A further category consists of people of either sex entering into mixed marriages, in the form of a refugee marrying a British-born partner. I do not believe it is possible to arrive at statistics about the distribution of sexes and the eventual success of these unions. Of the few I know, some are very happy, some less so – in other words no different from other marriages. Interestingly enough, though, I know of several cases where adverse effects caused by religious differences, which one would have thought could give rise to additional problems, were not only absent but, on the contrary, the non-Jewish British-born spouse converted to Judaism and, curiously enough, sometimes became the more 'practising' Jew of the two. Disregarding religion, what these marriages have in common is the automatic transplantation of a person from the refugee into the undiluted British community, irrespective of material and cultural considerations. This can undoubtedly be quite an uncomfortable culture shock even where the members of the British family accept the refugee without question. I remember a refugee friend of mine who married a lady, a member of an English-Jewish family. It was the second marriage for both partners. The union was distinctly happy and there was no trouble with the wife's family either. But he once confessed to me that for a long time he felt a comparative stranger with the latter and whenever he could, he invited the one remaining member of his own family to gatherings of the clans, so as to have some sort of a counterbalance.

Finally, let us not overlook the cases of refugees – practically always female – who married a Briton for no other reason than that he was 'genuinely English'. I know of several such cases, in which any objective observer could have seen at first glance that the prospective husband was in some ways very different or even inadequate and bound to cause the refugee partner to regret her rash step sooner rather than later. The position is perhaps not all that dissimilar from that of those British girls who married American GIs during the war. Forgetting shotgun weddings, not very common during that period anyway, the girls were often influenced by outward appearances and affluence. In quite a number of cases they soon realised their mistake but usually only after they had arrived in America after the war. The same excuse cannot be made for the refugee girls who married inadequate British men. They should have seen quite plainly what they were letting themselves in for, but to marry an 'echten Engländer' was so desirable a goal in itself that it blinded them – and sometimes their parents, who ought to have known better – to faults that were only too obvious.

However, all these cases are atypical exceptions. What I have said above applies to the majority of Hitler refugees.

V

If refugees, however innocently, are regarded in some ways as not on a par with British people, I'd like to hark back briefly to another rather aggravating discovery that I made in the course of my professional activities and to which I have already referred earlier in this book: the fact that a foreign national resident in Great Britain is regarded in a more unfavourable light than one living in his own country; and also – of particular importance to refugees – that someone living here voluntarily is more respected than a refugee living here by necessity. Far fetched? Let us look into this a little further.

The reasons, if my opinion is tenable, are again bound to be subconscious ones. A foreigner residing in a country not his own – as opposed to visiting it as a tourist – represents the 'foreign body' with all the reactions that implies and which I have already mentioned. The 'body' in this instance is the 'unit', the nation. 'They will take us over, destroy our national heritage!' Looked at in this way, a foreigner living here only temporarily, or for that matter a mere tourist, is not a 'foreign organ transplant', ie not a threat and is therefore more readily welcomed. And, coincidentally, the more foreign bodies there are milling around, the stronger the perceived threat and consequently the rejection. Admittedly, these opinions are usually underpinned by a number of realistic reasons: immigrants may increase crime and prostitution; take jobs away from natives; bleed 'the tax payer' – and what a wonderfully convenient animal that is – by taking up too much of the social services' funds; occupy hospital beds that should be reserved for nationals; and so on. All this is true and very often possesses a high degree of validity. But if this were all, most of these considerations would apply only to poor immigrants. Who can deny that there is also a prejudice against the wealthier ones? Indeed, I have sometimes found some sneaking, again subconscious, hostility in the case of, for instance, Indians or Pakistanis who were particularly successful in business and ended up as multi-millionaires. 'How come? Why them rather than us?' We even sometimes resent – or at least look down on with some pity – the newsagents belonging to these nationals working round the clock, something we would certainly accept with equanimity if we saw them do it in their own country.

But perhaps we may even go one step further? There is, as already mentioned, a none-too subtle difference between immigrants who left their country because they had to in order to escape persecution and those who come here of their own volition and live here permanently though they could go back to their country of origin at any time. I believe that for this reason the latter are seen as representing a lesser 'threat', but this is not the only point I want to make. It seems to me that a foreigner still accepted and backed by his own nation has a better standing in the eyes of the citizens of his host country than one without that support – provided he does have a country. Although anti-Semitism is certainly still with us in almost undiminished strength, I believe that it is in some circles far less bitter towards citizens of Israel than it used to be except, needless to say, in Arab countries. I sometimes wonder whether the position of gypsies would change if they had their own country to fall back on. They seem to think so, because they are apparently trying to establish a fictional one.

Coming back to the original Hitler refugees, I think it is arguable that the no-country-syndrome did add to our difficulties and to a certain extent perhaps still does. The fact, incidentally, that in theory we could now return to Germany and would be received there gladly (at least officially) does not make any great difference. For not only is this possibility not generally known even to refugees, but no-one in his right mind could seriously consider it feasible for most former German Jews to take such a step.

VI

With all these subtle influences it is small wonder that we felt and often still feel more comfortable among ourselves. And as already mentioned it was almost a matter of course that refugees would consult refugee doctors once these had received permission to practice. This was not only due to the language problem or the fact that the British system of division into general practitioners and specialists was quite strange to us. In Germany, if you had say, eczema, you could consult a skin specialist directly or if there was something wrong with your water works, a urologist. He might or might not have been recommended by your GP and would presumably keep in touch with him, but your GP had not 'referred' you to him. Some British specialists would not see you without such a referral. The German one carried out the necessary treatment himself instead of instructing the regular doctor what to do.

Apart from us not being used to the British way, it was again a matter of where you felt most comfortable and secure. There can, of course, not have been the slightest doubt that British GPs were every bit as good as refugee ones and often, presumably, better. They had closer connections than their German colleagues with top specialists and particularly surgeons. But this counted for very little. If there was a German, Austrian or whatever refugee doctor available – which was not always the case in smaller towns – he would be our first choice. The same applied to lawyers, accountants and similar professionals, though in their case there could be little doubt that their British colleagues had the advantage as far as knowledge of British law was concerned; on the other hand, they were not conversant with German or Austrian law, the knowledge of which was sometimes important.

One would assume that this tendency to consult refugees disappeared once we had been in this country for a few decades and to a large extent it has: not only because we have meanwhile become familiar with British ways, but also because the original generation of refugee doctors has for all practical purposes ceased to exist through effluxion of time. But we often still remember them with something near nostalgia. And I recall that when I asked an Alternative Health Society to send me a list of practitioners in my district, I had to stop myself, not without some amusement, from following my immediate and automatic inclination to consult the one with the most German-sounding name. By that time I had been living in this country for many decades, and yet my gut feeling had not changed.

VII

How can we sum up all this for our generation of refugees?
- We have managed to accept and conform to British ways to a considerable extent and are happy here.
- Consciously, the British, by and large, give us equal treatment, but we continue to be easily distinguishable, have not fully assimilated and therefore, sometimes subconsciously, are not completely accepted by the native population as 'one of them'.
- We for our part, notwithstanding our desires and efforts, have recognised the position, if not always consciously, and have accepted its consequences. We continue to conduct our main social intercourse in the environment where we feel most comfortable – with fellow refugees.

What follows? It is my belief that we original refugees shall never be fully integrated, nor do we still find this necessary. The halfway house that has evolved suits both parties: it has turned out to be the 'Happy Compromise' which is part of the title of this book.

"And do you also play the violin?"

by Carl F. Flesch

With rare humour and understanding, the author recounts his life as the son of a famous violinist. He describes the many artists and composers of world renown he has met, the problems of concert life, of being the son of a famous artist, and very much more. Lavishly illustrated with photos and facsimilies.

" *Of interest not only to violinists, musicologists and contemporary historians, but also to . . .the general reader."*
Sir Yehudi Menuhin in his foreword to the book

"Anyone interested in music and human beings will be fascinated by this extraordinary, delightful book." **The Spectator**

" The author writes with a personal detachment and analytical ability frequently absent from memoirs of artists themselves"
Classical Music

"Very readable, hard to put down (I had a hard job to wrest it from members of my family whilst trying to review it)" **ISM Journal**

"Valuable and interesting . . . never without a knowing chuckle..."
Die Presse, Austria

"Offers much material that has not been published before."
Musicology, Australia

"A veritable treasure trove . . . Casals, Kreisler, Schnabel, Furtwaengler, all pass through these pages . . . with letters filled with passion, acrimony, humour and grief . . . abounds with stories and anecdotes."
American String Teachers Association Magazine, USA

Published by Toccata Press, 1990
Hardback £17.50   Paperback £9.50
Obtainable post free from Pen Press Publishers Ltd
39-41 North Road, Islington, London N7 9DP   Tel: 020 7607 0517